THE HORSE AND THE BIT

Also by Susan McBane

Keeping a Horse Outdoors
Your First Horse: a guide to buying and owning
Keeping Horses: how to save time and money
Behaviour Problems in Horses
Ponywise
Effective Horse and Pony Management: a failsafe system
The Horse in Winter
The Competition Horse: its breeding, production and management
Practical Horsemastership (co-author/editor)
A Natural Approach to Horse Management
Horse Facts (co-author)
Pony Problems: how to cope
Understanding your Horse
All about your Pony

THE HORSE AND THE BIT

Edited by Susan M^CBane

First Edition

HOWELL
BOOK HOUSE
New York

First published in Great Britain in 1988
by The Crowood Press

Published in 1988 by Howell Book House Inc.
230 Park Avenue, New York, N.Y. 10169

© The Crowood Press 1988

Howell Book House
Macmillan Publishing Company
866 Third Avenue, New York, NY 10022
Collier Macmillan Canada, Inc.

Library of Congress Cataloging-in-Publication Data

The Horse and the bit.
   Includes index.
   Summary: Discusses the development of the bit and its
use in modern horseback riding.
   1. Bits (Bridles).   2. Bridles.   3. Horsemanship.
[1. Bits (Bridles).   2. Bridles.   3. Horsemanship]
I. McBane, Susan.
SF309.9.H66 1989   798.2   88-13509
ISBN 0-87605-878-0

Macmillan books are available at special discounts for bulk purchases
for sales promotions, premiums, fund-raising, or educational use.
For details, contact:

    Special Sales Director
    Macmillan Publishing Company
    866 Third Avenue
    New York, NY 10022

10 9 8 7 6 5 4 3 2

Acknowledgements

I should like to thank Hydrophane Laboratories Ltd. for the
photographs of the KK and Nathe German bits, and Joy Claxton
for her great patience and efficiency in producing the line drawings
which have so enhanced this book. The photographs in Chapter 5 are
reproduced by kind permission of *The Horse and Rider*. Fig 28 is by
Peter R. Sweet.

Typeset by Alacrity Phototypesetters, Weston-super-Mare
Printed and bound in Great Britain by
Butler & Tanner Ltd, Frome and London

Contents

Preface

May I begin by saying what this book is *not* intended to be? It is not meant to be an encyclopaedic reference work giving details of a stunning number and variety of bits, common or obscure, which the reader may wish to look up. Neither is it meant to be a conventional text book containing all the information already available in other books of that nature on bitting. For these two reasons, the book is also not intended for the beginner. It assumes a basic level of knowledge and offers a wide range of expert opinion for those wishing to build on that knowledge and explore the subject further.

The Horse and the Bit was purposely designed to be different. I specifically devised it to be a 'seminar in print', bringing together the opinions and advice of a fairly large number of experts, all of whom are highly competent in their chosen area of the horse world, on a subject which seems to cause endless fascination among horse enthusiasts. However, to accommodate the number of contributors to this book at a seminar and give them time to say what they do here would need a very expensive course lasting two or three days, even assuming they could all be available at the same time, which is unlikely.

I hope you will regard the book as one to be read and thought about, and subsequently dipped into for a 'refresher course', rather than as a reference source which is only used when needed. It is impossible to solve every problem or answer every query a reader may have in any book but I hope that the selection of topics chosen and presented here will go a long way towards promoting a better understanding of the subject to the mutual benefit of horses and humans.

There is, inevitably, some differing of opinion which will come as no surprise to anyone who has ever had instruction from more than one person or read more than one book on a subject but by different authors. Until the day arrives when living creatures are clones of each other within their species, there will always be many roads leading to Rome. Even clones, placed in different environments and given different experiences, may come up with different conclusions and opinions. Experts, being individuals, will always differ in their views.

Likewise, as some horses are more expert than others at coping with humans and their foibles, and all of them are as individual and idiosyncratic as we, both mentally and physically, we shall find that what works for one will be anathema to another.

Fashions come and go in every sphere, it seems, and bitting is no exception. Fifty years ago, polo ponies everywhere were played in double bridles or Pelhams almost to the exclusion of other bits. Today, the most common bitting arrangement seen on the polo field is the gag snaffle with a drop noseband that is too low and apparently too tight, a cavesson noseband and standing martingale, and sometimes a running martingale too! Twenty years ago, the Fulmer snaffle and drop noseband seemed to be all the rage for riding horses and many competition horses; it is much less common today when eggbutt and, increasingly, loose-ring snaffles seem to predominate.

Unfortunately, novice owners not uncommonly make the fatal mistake of choosing a particular bit and accoutrements for no better reason than that it *is* the current fashion. Perhaps they have spotted it in a tack shop and are intrigued by it, or have seen it on some famous horse or other and feel, therefore, that it must be good or even magic and is bound to turn their horse instantly into a world-beater.

There are two well-worn and true sayings in the horse world. One is: 'No foot, no horse'. The other is: 'There is a key to every horse's mouth'. If the originator of the latter saying meant that you only have to find the ideal bit and your horse will, by some shattering wizardry, be transformed into the perfectly behaved mount which always goes superbly at the lightest hint of an aid from you, then he did the horse (which has to endure the results of its owner's search for that key) a huge disservice.

A much more accurate interpretation of that saying is that the key does indeed exist, but, given a comfortable bit anyway, it is not so much the bit as the hands at the other end of the reins. It is the skill and sensitivity of the hands that operate the supposed key which really matter.

1 A History of Bits and Bitting

by Anthony Dent

The double bridle as we see it today in use on hunters, on police horses, on event horses and on the rapidly diminishing number of troop horses and chargers ridden by hide-and-hair cavalry, is about two centuries old. It evolved to its present form about the beginning of the Napoleonic Wars and there have been no basic modifications to it since that time. But its essential components, the snaffle or bridoon and the curb, are the culmination of a long period of trial and error that must have begun at the moment when men ceased to keep horses as we do cattle now, purely for milk and meat, but put them to work. And that would appear to be towards the end of the New Stone Age.

That moment occurred at a time when no metal was available to horsemen anywhere in the world, and when the first metal artefacts came on the scene they were of pure copper, which is too soft to make a workable bit and in any case would rapidly poison any animal that had one in its mouth for more than a very short time.

Domestication of the Horse

Taking for granted the usual assumption that the horse was the last of the major domesticated animals to be brought into the service of mankind, various means had been developed to control those animals already employed. These animals were, on the evidence of archaeology, the ass, the ox, the camel, the water buffalo, and perhaps also the reindeer. (The dog I exclude because it could only be driven, not ridden, and was and is controlled exclusively by voice.) The ass, in ancient times, was chiefly used for pack work, and commonly went bare-headed. When ridden, it was controlled by voice and the direction was given by tapping on the neck with a stick. The ox was controlled by means of a nose-ring, or a peg stuck through the septum which divides the nostrils – as was the water buffalo. The reindeer, when ridden (and there are still reindeer-riding tribes as well as reindeer-driving tribes in North Eurasia), was guided by reins attached to a loop that went round the base of the horns. The camel was not only led but ridden in a headstall, called in Arabic a *haqma*. When the Arabs, late by comparison with other

9

Asiatic peoples, first took to riding horses, they used a bitless bridle to which they gave the same name, which we have anglicised as 'hackamore'.

The exceptionally severe bits seen in Moroccan and Algerian bridles are not of Arabic origin but were introduced from Spain after the Arabian conquest of the Iberian peninsula, and eventually found their way to the Arabian homeland. The nose-ring/nose-peg device was obviously unsuited to the horse, though some archaeologists have misinterpreted certain ancient pictures from Sumeria (Iraq) as showing horses controlled by nose-rings. Closer study of other pictures shows this not to be so – what they actually show is a muzzle, and the animal is not a horse but an onager (Asiatic wild ass). These animals bite furiously – ask any zoo keeper – and had to be muzzled at work. A simple solution was to fit a ring to the front end of the muzzle, and reins to the ring.

This device was developed no further because as soon as the Sumerians came into possession of horses, which did not *automatically* bite anything and anybody within reach, they found another solution. A solitary example of the ass-riding technique applied to the horse was seen in antiquity among the Numidians of North Africa, where asses were first domesticated, but where no wild horse ever lived. When the domesticated horse was introduced into Numidia from Spain, at a time we cannot determine but probably after 1000 BC, the locals took to the new mount like ducks to water, but they rode horses without any headgear at all, only a strap round the neck to act as brake and a fine switch to apply directional aids to the neck.

Development of the Bit

The final solution, owing nothing to devices previously in use on other species, was the bit, and all the evidence (as well as the lack of evidence) goes to show that it was the discovery of a people well outside what the ancients considered the civilised world – outside the Mediterranean region and the 'Bible lands' of the Near East, among the nomads of the steppes somewhere between the Black Sea and Mongolia. These people had plenty of 'ornamental' metals – copper, silver, even gold – but no iron, no tin to mix with their copper to make hard bronze. The bits they made consisted of twisted rawhide mouthpieces between cheekpieces of stag-horn.

None of these mouthpieces have survived, but cheekpieces of horn are quite plentiful among archaeological discoveries in the Ukraine, for instance. Although all the rawhide mouthpieces that went with them rotted away thousands of years ago (at best they must have been as expendable as throw-away razors), such is the conservatism of craftsmen that the first metal snaffles were made in exact imitation of these – the bronze was cast in a 'barley-sugar' shape mould to simulate the twisted thongs. The tradition is not quite dead today; you will occasionally see new snaffles made to this pattern, for no practical reason. The overall design of ancient bridles was dictated by the stag-horn cheekpiece, even after this, too, had become bronze or even iron. These too were sometimes cast with a 'rustic' finish to simulate the horn. There was no noseband, both sidepieces of the bridle being Y-shaped, the forks terminating in holes at either end of the cheekbars.

The oldest complete bits – or those

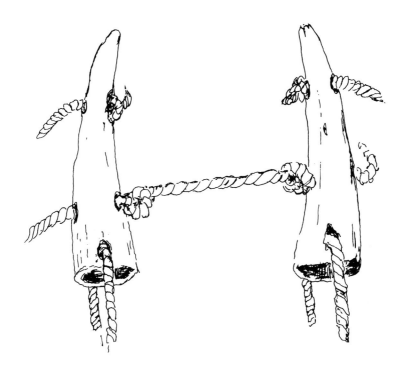

Fig 1   Reconstruction drawing of a twisted rawhide mouthpiece with stagshorn sidepieces.

complete enough to be able to tell what they would have looked like in their entirety – come from the Ukraine, north of the Black Sea, and can be dated to about 1500 BC. They are of bronze. At this date, European horsemen hardly rode at all; the entire Western World was dominated by a chariot-driving aristocracy which was slowly extending its influence westwards and northwards towards the Atlantic and the Baltic coasts. Every bit dating from this period, then, will have been for driving purposes.

Later, especially in the Iron Age, riding came to be more and more widely practised, but there was no such thing as a bit for driving and a bit for riding. Typical of specimens found in the British Isles are a pair buried with a charioteer and his chariot at Garton Slack in the East Riding of Yorkshire in the second or third century BC and excavated in 1971. Their discoverer, Tony Brewster, then County Archaeologist to what is now North Humberside, described them thus:

'... one was broken in two and the other one was complete. Both were identical and were of the three-linked type with rigid rein-rings welded on to the side mouthpieces at an angle of roughly 90°. The mouthpieces consisted of two side links joined together by a central link. This central hourglass-shaped link was bound round the centre by a narrow band which had been hammered round it. Bits of this type are rather fierce ...'

11

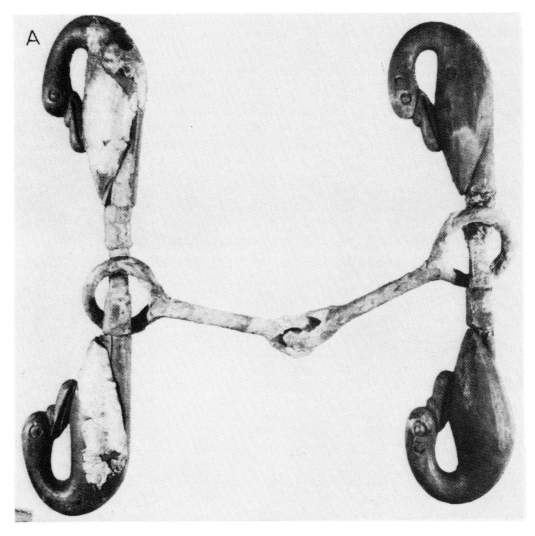

Fig 2   A bit from the third barrow of the archaeological site at Pazyryk in the eastern Altai mountains, excavated between 1947 and 1949 by the Russian anthropologist S.I. Rudenko. The cheekpieces are carved like ducks' heads.

They were of iron, but at this date bits were just as likely to be of bronze, as they had been for many centuries. In Britain, all were essentially snaffles, but the mouthpiece could be in one, two or even three sections, as above. Of course, the jointed kind produced a nutcracker action on the jaw if clumsily applied. The 'solid bar' type usually had a straight mouthpiece. Occasionally this was slightly bowed, though never so much as to produce anything like the effect of a port.

I have seen one such bit, labelled 'North-eastern Gaul, 2nd century BC', that looked exactly like what is now called a dressage Weymouth.

The only way of telling whether a bit found in isolation was for riding or driving is by the cheekpieces. These, whether in the form of rings or bars, were the same at either end if used for riding, but in the case of a pair for driving the outer ends were larger and more elaborate, sometimes taking the form of animal or even human figures.

The Curb

Something along the lines of a curb appeared in the Roman Empire, at various points, and the design is thought to have originated in Gaul, though none have so far been found in Britain. This early curb consisted not of a port or any sort of elaboration of the mouthpiece, but of a plain snaffle with bars at either end which were joined below the jaw by a metal rod immediately under the bars of the mouth. When the rein tightened the jaw was pinched between this rod and the mouthpiece of the bit. This, in the end, proved counter-productive because it was almost impossible to avoid squeezing the tongue, with disastrous after-effects. A different solution was found, first by devising a mouthpiece that consisted of two cones joined in the middle, thus giving more room to the tongue, and secondly by the invention of the curb chain instead of the under-jaw rod. This last variation was a Hungarian invention, but no examples earlier than the sixteenth century have been found.

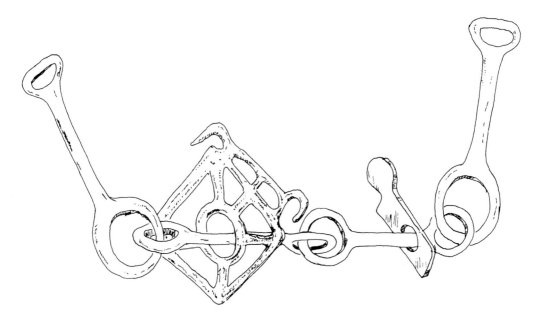

Fig 3   A bit for the nearside horse of a chariot pair, the left end more elaborate.

13

This early type of curb bit remained essentially the same throughout medieval Europe, with minor variations, mainly for knights in battle (though all the time the snaffle continued to be used for other purposes). Because the knight was confined in an increasingly unyielding straitjacket of armour, his left arm burdened with a shield and his right holding a weapon, he needed a bit that would produce instant reaction at the slightest shift of his bridle hand – or so the military historians say.

How comes it, then, that when High School riding began in the fifteenth or sixteenth century in Spain and Naples,

the cavalier who was no longer on a battle field (nor on a field at all), was not wearing armour and wielded only a 'riding rod' which admittedly was long enough to go fishing with if he got bored with riding, provided himself with bits that were even more elaborate, more mouth-cramming, more compulsive than ever before? The sheer weight of ironmongery illustrated in such books as Blundeville's *Fower Chiefest Ofyces* is daunting.

The limits of compulsion were reached, in England, under Henry VIII. As the reign of Queen Elizabeth wore on, as French replaced Italian influence, milder

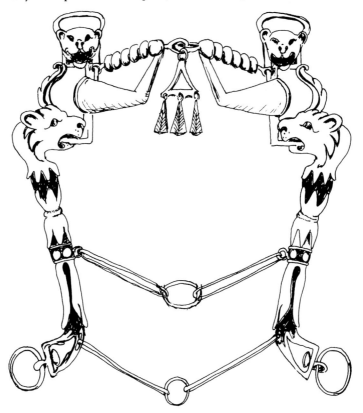

Fig 4 *'The sheer weight of ironmongery illustrated in such books as Blundeville's* Fower Cheifest Ofyces *is daunting.'*

forms of curb were introduced, and this trend continued through the seventeenth century. Equestrian portraits of both men and women, in that century and the next, frequently show two reins, which might lead you to think that a double bridle is in use. But this is never the case. The two reins are attached to the same bit – one to the end of the cheekpiece and one to its centre, where it joins the mouthpiece and has a mild action similar to that of a snaffle. These reins were never used together – as long as a high, narrow pommel was in use, the disengaged rein was simply looped over it, where it can be seen hanging loosely.

The Double Bridle

Some time in the 1780s or 1790s the true double bridle was born, in which curb and snaffle were united after many centuries of independent existence. The snaffle (or bridoon, or watering bit) had to be much thinner than previously, to ensure that the mouth was not unduly stuffed with metal, and the Hungarian invention of the curb chain was also incorporated. This was the last really revolutionary change of design for riding bridles and it came about from the increasing employment of Thoroughbred or at least half-bred horses for purposes other than racing. But to this day double bridles are rarely seen in Spain because the Iberian peninsula alone in Western Europe escaped the general Anglomania of which the most striking manifestations were the Thoroughbred (*le pursang anglais*), and the top hat (*le haut-de-forme*).

Early Bit-Making

Things are not always what they seem when it comes to interpreting ancient parts of lorinery. Many snaffles of classical antique date have at their ends, inside the rein-ring, a metal disc with projections on the inner side which have been interpreted as 'thorns' to force the head to one side when the rein on that side is pulled. In fact, they are only there to prevent the bit sliding through the mouth, and the projections have the opposite purpose. The discs were lined on the inner side with leather to prevent chafing, and the 'thorns' were the means of fixing this lining in place. Of course, if these spikes had really come into contact with the corners of the mouth, they would have caused severe abrasions and very soon rendered the horse unrideable.

That the bit-making trade was once a very important one is evident from its very specialisation. A man of this craft could make a good living by making *nothing but* bits and indeed, by the rules of his guild, he was forbidden to make anything else for sale. The old English name for this calling was bridlesmith (the man who made the leather parts was called a bridle-*cutter*), to be duplicated after the Norman conquest by the borrowed French word *lorimer*, and for a long time the two words existed side by side. Like spurrier, also a very exclusive craft, both became hereditary surnames, but the name Lorimer soon became confused with Loriner (meaning 'the man from Lorraine') so that many families alternated in spelling and pronunciation back and forth every few generations.

North America

About 1700, the whole man/horse confrontation was acted out all over again in another continent but in an environment closely resembling the North Eurasian steppe where the equestrian story began. At that date, the Plains Indians of North America first came across appreciable numbers of feral horses, descendants of runaways from the Spanish settlements in Mexico. These mustangs, over the generations, had migrated thousands of miles north, at least as far as Lake Winnipeg and the Canadian border, but had not turned one pace right, into the forests, or left into the Rocky Mountains. They simply followed the grass.

The Indians had one advantage over their counterparts in the prehistoric Mongolian steppe. Though they had never seen it, they knew, from travellers' tales, that somewhere, far to the east, the Palefaces had learned the secret of persuading this new animal *Shonk-a-Wakon*, the Magic Dog, to carry them around as a squaw carried a papoose. Otherwise they were worse off than the first horsemen of the Old World – like them, they had only stone and bone tools and weapons, but unlike them they had no experience of domestic animals of any kind except the dog. However, they had the lasso, and an innate skill in hunting.

The secret they learned for themselves, not from the Palefaces, and their solution for controlling the Magic Dog was simply to tie a loop around its lower jaw and from this another thong passing back over the withers and forward again to the jaw. This was the Indian bridle, and it sufficed for all purposes for at least a hundred years – no real attempt was made to improve it. In time they acquired from the Palefaces bits for which they fashioned their own bridles, but meanwhile there were no bone or horn snaffles. George Catlin in *Manners ... of the North American Indians*, 1841, recalls meeting a band of Comanches in the course of his travels along the Mexican border whose leader had no saddle but a 'heavy Spanish bit' which Catlin assumed was booty from some encounter with the Mexicans.

2 Manufacture of Bits

by Ron Etherington

In the past, when a bit-maker manufactured a bit, he would consider the seven classical points of control, then, using the basic principles of levers and fulcrums, he would make a bit which would apply pressure to one or more of these points, hopefully making allowances for safety and comfort. Today, with few exceptions, bits are mass-produced to classical designs by engineers who are seldom horsemen. This can and sometimes does mean items appearing on the market that are totally unsuitable.

The responsible bit-maker chooses a material that should be durable, and a method of construction based on sound engineering principles. He also takes care when assembling cheeks to mouths to ensure a smooth joint in order that no pinching occurs, thus causing damage in the horse's mouth.

Correct fitting of bits is essential and it is the responsibility of the bit-maker to make a full range of sizes. It is normal to make mouths from $3\frac{1}{2}$in, in increments of $\frac{1}{4}$in up to 6in, although on occasions, larger sizes can be required. Curb and Pelham cheeks commence at 4in and increase in $\frac{1}{2}$in increments up to 7in, and up to 9in in the case of harness bits. Rings should be manufactured in $\frac{1}{8}$in increments in their internal ring size and can vary from 1in to $3\frac{1}{2}$in. This should ensure a range of sizes which will result in correct fitting for all horses.

When producing jointed mouth bits, care should be taken to ensure that the action is centralised. The parts used in a jointed mouth are called the Upperton (male) and the Pearston (female). If both of these parts are made the same size, the pivot point will not be in the centre of the mouth, and therefore the action will be uneven. This is easily identified by folding the bit and checking that the cheeks are parallel – if not the bit will be rendered useless. Occasionally this 'mistake' will be accentuated to make an anti-lugging bit. This is a bit where the pivot action is moved to an off-centre position in order to give a greater amount of leverage to one side of the bit. Other than on this occasion, however, the action must be central. Thickness of mouths also changes the action of the bit: in general the thicker the mouth the gentler the action, and conversely the thinner the mouth the sharper the action.

Materials

Bits have changed little over their many years of use. However, there have been several noticeable improvements in recent years, and whilst much is made of the quality of bit-making in past ages, recent improvements in manufacturing methods suggest that we are standing at the doorway of an exciting future. Over the years, bit-making has used the techniques and materials available to that period and, therefore, many early forms of bitting were crude in both their manufacturing techniques and the materials used. There were, however, some notable exceptions. The materials used both historically and at present can be divided into metals and non-metals. Metals used vary little throughout the world and the following are some of the more common.

Iron

Often malleable cast iron, this material is usually nickel or chromium plated. It is very strong, cheap and wears well but usually rusts and has lost much of its popularity in recent years.

Brass

Again, usually nickel or chromium plated, brass is not generally considered strong enough for bit-making and wears very quickly. It is a little more expensive than iron but whilst it is not liable to rust, the plating does tend to flake. This material has never been very popular but is still used in some parts of the world.

Solid Nickel

This is a euphemism – the correct description is nickel silver, being an alloy of brass and nickel. It usually has a 12 – 14 per cent nickel content and was extremely popular until quite recently. If well made, it is usually considered strong enough but tends to yellow with age, and joints can wear quite quickly. Due to a general decline in quality (it is a difficult material with which to obtain consistently good results), it tends to be less popular.

Other Nickel Alloys

These are usually cupro-nickel alloys (a mixture of copper and nickel) with a 40 per cent nickel content, and are sold under well-known brand names. This material is very strong and wears extremely well. It has a strong blue-white colour. It is more expensive, reflecting the considerably higher cost of the material used, and it maintains its finish and colour for a long time. It has traditionally been used for the finest quality bits.

Stainless Steel

In its finest form it should be an 18/8 stainless steel. It is very strong and rust-free, with a grey/white colour. Articles manufactured in this material are similar in price to cupro-nickel bits, in this case reflecting the considerable cost in working with a relatively cheap but difficult material. This type of steel was unknown prior to 1940 and manufacturers working with it have to be extremely careful of contamination problems. There have been numerous cases of problems caused by quite small amounts of contaminants infiltrating into the material during the manufacture of bits, resulting in breakage.

Other Metals

Certain other metals are used in specific instances.

Aluminium   This is used for lightness in certain circumstances but great care should be taken because of its weakness, particularly as it is used extensively in racing.

Aluminium Bronze   A yellow metal

usually used for decorative purposes, this is especially popular for driving bits. It is very strong but exceedingly difficult to work with.

Copper This orange-coloured metal is not considered very strong, and it is also very expensive. Used mainly in the construction of mouths, it has good mouthing qualities.

Non-Metals

A number of other materials are used particularly for mouth construction.

Wood This is still used occasionally but is usually supported by metal inserts, to give strength and security.

Rubber This is a very popular material particularly when used with a chain insert, which gives flexibility with safety.

Ebonite Preformed on a metal insert using heat and pressure, as in vulcanising, this is an extremely popular and successful material. However, as true ebonite is difficult to obtain, pseudo-alternatives tend to be used more often which are not always as successful.

Leather In the early days a simple bit would be constructed using a leather strap with a ring at either end. Today leather is used merely as a cover, usually over a metal mouth, in order to increase softness, often with surprisingly good results.

Synthetics Various new synthetic materials are becoming available as a result of discoveries in the petro-chemical industry, and some very good results

appear to be achieved, particularly with regard to flexibility and strength.

Methods

The metals used in bit-making may be worked with a variety of methods with varying degrees of success.

Forging

This is the traditional method of bit production and in its finest form produced bits of outstanding quality. The material was heated in a forge and the craftsman then worked with a variety of tools shaping the individual pieces of a bit, in a manner similar to a blacksmith. Unfortunately, I know of no one who is capable of producing work by this method, to a satisfactory standard, today.

Casting

This is the most commonly used method and most of the bits produced are made this way. The principle is that metal is melted in a furnace and then poured into a mould representing the shape required. When cooling, the metal assumes that shape. The usual technique is for the mould to be formed in sand by pressing the sand around a pattern of the article required. This method is used for lower temperature materials such as brass, solid nickel and cupro-nickel. Although a number of technical problems can arise, in general this technique is usually successful.

For the higher temperatures required by materials such as stainless steel, traditional techniques of moulding, as outlined above, are rarely consistently successful, and if used lead to quality problems. However, there are techniques such as lost wax casting (sometimes known as investment casting), hot box and cold box techniques that use synthetic sand, which are capable of withstanding the required temperatures. The principles of some of these techniques have been known for a long time, but their use in bit-making is a recent innovation.

Fabricating

This technique of bit-making owes much to modern welding methods and is well proven in both the aircraft and motor industry. It has been used extensively in bit-making in America for some 20 years. Its introduction into English steel bits has been slow but the results spectacular. The technique involves forming stainless steel parts of quite simple shape and then welding them together. This method is used particularly for hollow mouth bits, where two 'shell' shapes are formed on a press and then seamed together, resulting in a very strong light mouth shape which hitherto could only be formed by a complicated and not always successful moulding method.

The above three techniques are all usually followed by a variety of grinding and polishing techniques in order to give a smooth and attractive surface finish, sometimes by the use of automatic machines but often by hand polishing. In addition, a variety of cold forming, turning and winding operations may be used during final assembly.

Suitability

The manufacture of bits is practised in many parts of the world today by producers who have no real knowledge of the ways in which the bits are to be used. Classical designs of bits have evolved over many centuries and the development problems have passed into history. However, with new innovations and attempts at new designs, often with insufficient test and development time given, problems are encountered. Differing manufacturing techniques and materials are available today but problems still remain when considering abrasive resistance and cold weather behaviour.

When the rider is selecting the correct bit for a particular problem, he is faced with a difficult task. First he must choose a style and shape to achieve the action he requires, then he must obtain the correct size, and finally, a quality that is safe and sure. It is impossible in a work of this nature to list all of the pitfalls, and the safest course must be to purchase a bit from a reputable saddler. Most importantly, buy a bit which is indelibly marked by its manufacturer. This unfortunately is not as widely done as might be imagined, but should ensure, in the event of failure, a proven responsibility. With the variety of uses and shapes available, no one method suits all situations, but the most important development appears to be the ability of the modern bit-maker to use combinations of materials and methods enumerated above in order to make a satisfactory bit. For instance, the producer who is able to fabricate a whole mouth and assemble it to an investment casting cheek, using a rust-free material and following proven techniques, is today able to produce a product of a quality hitherto not available. However, great care needs to be taken when changing techniques of manufacture, to ensure that the product is safe. Some notable failures have resulted in recent years where apparently the best techniques and materials have been used, but with hindsight, have been totally inappropriate when considering the use of the product.

3 The Horse's Mouth

by R. J. Fisher, BVSc., MRCVS

Structure of the Teeth

The teeth are of three basic types. The incisor teeth are simple elongated cutting teeth situated at the front of the mouth and used, in conjunction with the lips, to take food into the mouth. They have little importance in relation to bit problems. Canine teeth or tushes are elongated tapering teeth with very long roots, situated behind the incisors and, again, well away from the bit. The cheek teeth or molars and premolars are the teeth most relevant in causing bitting problems and are also most frequently subject to disease. They require frequent dental attention. They are roughly cube shaped with a series of hard enamel folds containing softer cement lakes, the whole having an uneven surface or table for grinding. Because the cement is softer than the surrounding enamel, food may accumulate at these sites and lead to periodontal disease. The incisors and cheek teeth of the horse continue to grow throughout most of life to replace tooth worn away by constant grinding of opposing surfaces.

The role played by the teeth in influencing problems relating to the bit largely results from the relative positions of the teeth and the bit. Consequently the most important teeth to be involved are the first upper cheek teeth and, where present, the wolf teeth.

Position of the Teeth

The arrangement of the permanent teeth within the horse's mouth consists, at the lips, of three pairs of incisor teeth in each jaw. Behind these lie a pair of canines in each jaw, one tooth on each side. Canine teeth are more frequently present in males but can be present in mares and are particularly common in the lower jaw or mandible. Their position in the space between the incisors and the cheek teeth (in the diastema or 'bars') is variable but usually the upper canines lie approximately midway along the bars of the mouth, whereas the lower canines are closer to the incisors. The bit lies between the canines and the cheek teeth, on the bars, and is usually well away from the canines which consequently do not cause bitting problems. The cheek teeth comprise three pairs of permanent molar teeth at the back of each jaw, in front of which lie three more pairs of temporary premolars. Temporary premolars are replaced by permanent teeth at two and a half years of age in the case of the first two pairs, and three and a half years for the third pair. Occasionally during this period the temporary tooth may become firmly lodged as a sharp cap on the top of the erupting permanent tooth, causing irritation and requiring physical removal.

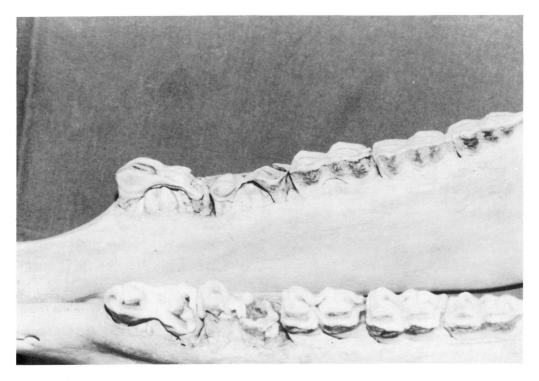

*Fig 5   Caps on the premolar teeth may cause discomfort in
young horses.*

Wolf Teeth

In front of the premolars in the upper jaw a pair of vestigial wolf teeth may or may not be present. The significance of wolf teeth as a cause of resistance to the bit by a horse is controversial. Undoubtedly their presence is frequently blamed where poor riding is the fault but they can, and do, cause problems. Although they are often unexpectedly small, frequently being less than one centimetre in length, with very short roots, wolf teeth are important because they are situated immediately in front of the premolars, exactly where the bit would normally sit. Trouble arises when one or both are angled or slightly out of alignment. A problem is manifested by the horse turning its head away from the problem tooth while moving forward, and leaning on the bit on the affected side; that is, hanging away from the affected side. Since the roots of wolf teeth are very short, they are easily removed and it is probably easier to remove them and be sure that they are not causing any mouth problem which may have arisen. Removal is usually carried out whilst the horse is standing, using a specially designed punch or dental elevator.

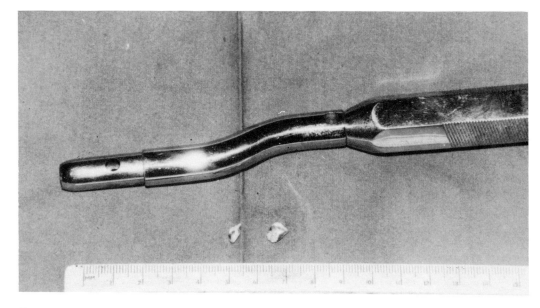

*Fig 6   Wolf teeth (first premolar) and extractor. The extractor
fits over the tiny tooth and by tilting, the tooth is easily
removed.*

Problems caused by Cheek Teeth

Sharp front upper cheek teeth may cause the horse to resist the bit. Taking a section across the horse's nose at the level of the first cheek teeth, you will see that the space between the lower dental arcades or rows is thirty per cent smaller than that between the upper arcades. Since, during eating, the teeth move over each other in a circular motion from front to back in contrast to the side-to-side motion of the cow, an area on the outside of the upper teeth and the inside of the lower teeth is not worn. As a result a sharp edge is formed along the length of the arcade. In the case of the upper teeth this sharp edge may damage the inside of the cheek, particularly when pressure is put on the outside of the cheek by the cheek straps and the bit.

Discomfort is further exacerbated when the lower jaw is undershot so that the upper and lower arcades are not vertically aligned. Wear is not complete and a pointed beak may be formed on the first upper premolar. It is important to have the teeth properly checked and, where necessary, rasped at least twice a year until five years of age, and at least annually thereafter. Teeth problems occur more rapidly in horses that are housed and fed hard feed than in those on grass, so it is sensible to have the teeth checked before turning out for a period of grazing. Since the teeth are continually growing and continually being ground away at the top, sharp edges will continue to form. If a cheek tooth should be lost, the tooth opposite to it may not be

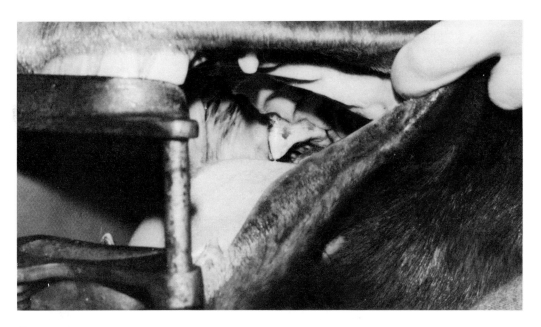

Fig 7 *A hook on upper premolar 2 which may interfere with the bit. When present, the wolf tooth sits immediately in front of this tooth. Note that the canine teeth are well forward and should not interfere with the bit.*

Fig 8 *Rasp blades come in a variety of forms.*

properly worn away, creating special problems.

Usually abnormalities of the incisor teeth do not cause problems in association with the bit, nor do canine teeth unless they are abnormally close to the cheek teeth.

Diseases of Teeth

Cavities or dental caries, as occur in man, occur in the cheek teeth of horses but are rarely detected clinically. Periodontal disease (pyorrhoea) is common in the horse and increases with age, seventy-five per cent of horses over 15 years of age being affected. It may follow gingivitis (inflammation of the gums) after food has become impacted and degraded at the base of the teeth, or following damage to the cement lakes in the centre of the cheek teeth. Once the central pulp becomes inflamed and infected, an abscess may develop producing swelling on the face or the lower jaw, difficulty in eating and sometimes a purulent discharge from one nostril. These are often the first signs of dental disease and are comparatively rare. Treatment at this stage is usually complex and may involve surgery under general anaesthesia.

Wounds within the Mouth

Because the mouth has a very good blood supply, soft tissue wounds within the mouth heal remarkably quickly and completely. This is even more surprising considering that non-sterile food is continuously in contact with the wound causing further superficial damage. Even fractures of the jaws heal rapidly once the fracture has been immobilised so that there is no movement between the broken ends of bone. Clearly, while an open wound is still present the horse will resent having any form of restraining device placed within the mouth. Furthermore, the rapid rate of wound healing is no excuse for the neglect of wounds within the mouth. Many oral wounds are caused by the effects of an improperly fitting or used bit, but anything damaging the surface of the mucous membrane will establish a wound which will remain until left alone long enough for it to heal completely. The corners of the lips are particularly difficult sites as they are continually rubbed by the overlying bit. Most frequently a wound here results from a headstrong horse pulling against the bit or the bit being held too high in the mouth. Once a painful site is established, the horse fails to respond to pressure on the bit and, by fighting for the pressure to be relieved, further increases the severity of the wound.

Occasionally mouth wounds may arise from eating something sharp, or be secondary to the presence of warts, in the younger horse, or a flat verrucose skin tumour, the sarcoid. Mild skin cracks may be protected using Vaseline or a mild antiseptic salve. Warts regress over a period of a few weeks to several months, but sarcoids do not disappear spontaneously and require surgical procedures to remove them, of which cooling to a very low temperature (cryosurgery) is probably the most successful. Where the wound is too severe to allow a bit to be used, consider using a bitless bridle.

Excessively severe use of the bit can also result in bruising of the bars of the mouth and in this case adequate rest is the only successful answer to treatment. Depending on the severity of the bruising, recovery may take several weeks to complete.

Occasionally wounds are found under the chin where a curb chain has been too tightly applied. Such a problem should be recognised in the early stages since the initial swelling that occurs will cause more severe damage from the curb chain. Damage then progresses to an open wound, and finally to fibrous tissue being laid down and a permanent hard bony thickening. If a curb chain must be used where damage is present, it is best sheathed in a rubber protector or a sheepskin sleeve.

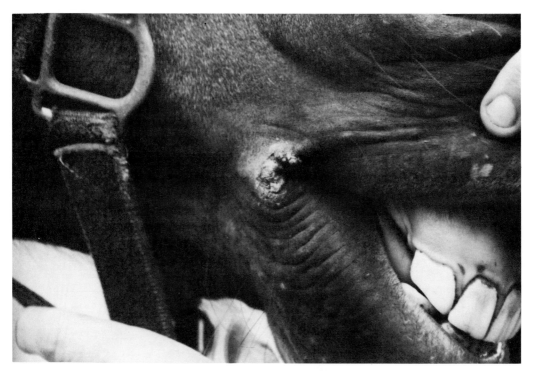

Fig 9 Warts on the commisure (corners) of the lips of a four-year-old. They caused soreness and resistance to the bit until they spontaneously regressed.

Lampas

Lampas is a condition which has in the past been regarded as pathological but which has for many years been recognised by the observant horseman as a state that is normally present in the young horse. When the temporary upper incisor teeth are being replaced by permanent incisors there is a period during which the soft tissues between the mucous membranes and the hard palate of the roof of the mouth just behind the incisors protrudes below the level of the newly erupting teeth. Abrasion by feeds may cause this to become inflamed, resulting in discomfort in the mouth in horses between two and a half and four years of age. However, the teeth rapidly grow down to protect the area and no treatment is required other than to avoid feeding whole cereals with sharp awns, or very coarse hay. A straight metal or rubber bit or a half moon bit is helpful to keep the pressure away from the sensitive area.

Reaction to Pain in the Mouth

The horse's reaction to pain in its mouth depends largely on the severity of the pain. Where the pain is long-standing, the horse will become headshy and appre-

27

hensive. It is then difficult to handle the mouth, or to place a bit in the mouth without the horse becoming distressed and placing his nose as far out of reach as possible.

Where pain is very mild, as may result from the application of pressure on a curb chain or the action of the central plate of a Dr Bristol bit, then the horse will submit to such a signal and fulfil the rider's wish.

If the pain is more severe, however, as, for example, when the aid is applied at a site where there is a wound, then the horse responds by resisting the infliction of pain. Contrary to the expected response of drawing away from the painful site, the horse will actually apply constant pressure over the painful area. Probably, this prompts the release of the naturally produced opiates, encephalins and endorphins. The effect is much the same as the relief obtained by pressing on an aching tooth to relieve pain. This response is seen where there is a continuous dull ache or low grade pain, such as discomfort produced by the presence of a misplaced wolf tooth in contact with the bit.

It is important that the bit should be the correct size for the horse. A jointed snaffle that is too small will pinch the corners of the mouth, producing painful wounds and further discomfort. If the bit is too large it will produce a sharp angle at

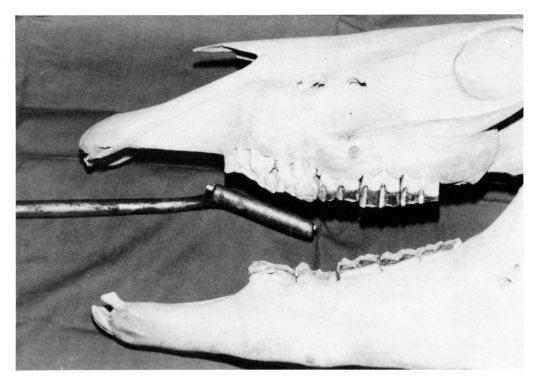

Fig 10   Use of angled rasp to remove sharp edges on the upper premolar teeth.

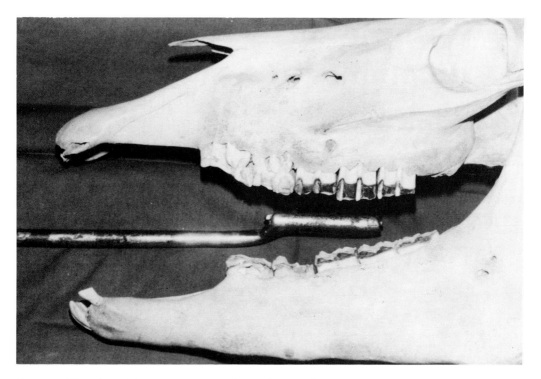

Fig 11   Use of straight rasp to remove sharp edges on the lower cheek teeth and the upper molars.

the joint, which puts greater pressure on the roof of the mouth. This point should be borne in mind especially when considering the Arabian horse, which has a long tapering nose with only a short distance between the bars of the mouth. In these animals it is probably wise to use only a straight or half moon bit.

When a sudden acute pain is experienced, the response by the horse is altogether different from the response to low grade pain. Under this circumstance he becomes restless and anxious and behaviour may progress to rearing or plunging. In this case the cause of pain can be quickly identified.

29

4 Gaining an Independent Seat

by Dési Lorent

'Only a rider with a proper position can obtain valid results from his horse.' This sentence is the very first one in the opening chapter of Master Nuno Oliveira's excellent book *Reflections on Equestrian Art*. The fact that the Master, who is considered to be the greatest classical rider of this century, and who has trained innumerable horses and riders, puts that sentence at the beginning of his book should make the rider understand how indispensable that position is. It is absolutely mandatory for all riders. Master Oliveira defines it perfectly in a few lines:

The academic [classical] position is the only one which allows you independence and finesse of the aids.
The shoulders should be straight and low.
The tummy is pushed towards the ears of the horse.
The bottom must not protrude behind a vertical line dropped from the shoulders.
The coccyx lies close to the pommel.
The thighs descend as vertically as possible with relaxed muscles.
There is supple articulation, the calf lightly in contact.
The head is in line with the neck and shoulders.

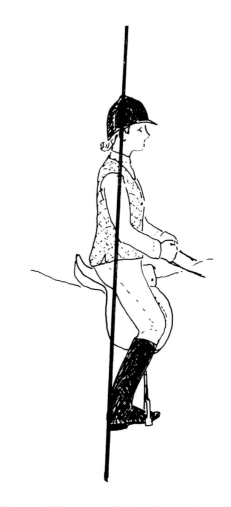

Fig 12   The correct, balanced classical seat. An imaginary line falls through the rider's ear, shoulder, elbow, hip and heel.

He also says that it is not enough for the position to be elegant – it must also be efficient. He strongly emphasises the fact that the body must remain in accordance with the movement of the horse.

Without a truly secure and independent seat of this nature, it is impossible for the hands themselves to be independent, able to be used by the rider with finesse, accuracy and precision no matter what bit is used and no matter what the rest of the rider's body or the horse is doing. Indeed, without such a seat it is likely that the hands will do harm by acting, with or without the rider's intention, in the wrong way or at the wrong time, misdirecting, confusing and probably hurting the horse.

Until a rider has learned this type of seat on the flat, he cannot expect to achieve a secure, balanced seat over fences. The points made in this chapter are based on the tuition I received from Master Oliveira over many years and on my own work and study.

The classical position is easy to explain when talking about a static position, but the difficulty lies in keeping a dynamic position, in other words, maintaining that position on a moving horse. For this, you must develop balance and co-ordination, both of which rely entirely on the position and which later lead to the independence of the aids. If you sit in the proper position the horse can carry you with ease and comfort. If you are out of position, out of harmony with it, its task is much more difficult and strenuous.

If you ever go to a circus and watch any balancing act, you will see that the performers all have an ideal position which allows them to use their bodies with precision and finesse, with no over-controlling which would be detrimental to their balance. Riders who grip with any part of the body to try and stay with the horse upset the balance and disturb the equilibrium of the horse, which in turn makes riding uncomfortable and more difficult. But when a rider and horse work in harmony and establish a good relationship, the result is quality equitation.

Muselaire talks a lot in his book, *Equitation*, about the importance of the back – the small of the back – and the necessity for the rider to establish a good dialogue between his own back and that of the horse. He also explains that with real equestrian tact more is performed through the back than the hand.

To make this clear, the way the horse's body and legs move during its various gaits must be understood, so that the rider may, in turn, understand how to use his body during each gait so that he truly goes *with* his horse, and is in harmony with it rather than hindering it.

The Walk

We often hear that the walk is a four-time, lateral gait, the horse moving each pair of legs on one side of its body alternately – that is, right hind, right fore, then left hind, left fore. But what is never explained, it seems, is that its back, too, is moving laterally. As the right legs are moving forward, the right side of the back moves slightly forward, too; consequently, the rider's back must also move laterally if he is to stay in harmony with his horse. Therefore, as the right side of the horse's body is moving forward the rider's right seatbone moves forward a fraction with it in time with the right hindleg, and as the left side moves forward, the left seatbone similarly is moved slightly forward. There is no need to move the seatbones backwards again as the rider will find that this occurs naturally without effort from him.

The Trot

At trot, the horse's legs move in diagonal pairs. As the left hind leg and right foreleg move forward (this is called the right diagonal) the left side of the horse's back will become hollow, and vice versa. At the same time, the left diagonal (right hind, left fore) is moving backwards; as the right hind hits the ground and pushes off again the right side of the horse's back rises slightly.

Sitting Trot

In sitting trot the seatbones absorb as completely as possible the rhythm and movement transferred to them through the horse's back. The small of the rider's back moves forward and down as each diagonal pair of legs hits the ground, and backward and up as the suspension phase between diagonals occurs and the horse is off the ground. The only conscious movement on the part of the rider is the forward-and-down movement; the natural momentum of the pace brings about the upward-and-back movement without any effort by the rider.

The seatbones are consciously, but without force, pushed under by the rider to maintain them in correct and constant contact with the deepest part of the saddle.

Rising Trot

Here, the seat remains pushed gently under the body, the back is straight and flat and the body inclined slightly forward of the vertical. The rise is more a

Fig 13   The correct, balanced position for sitting trot.

forward than an upward movement. This is the only way not to be left behind the movement. I often see riders who do rising trot with much too vertical a position and one that is out of harmony with the movement of the horse. The rider is consequently unbalanced and often has to grip with both hand and leg to raise himself out of the saddle.

The Canter

If a horse is cantering with, say, the off fore leading, the right side of his body is carried slightly in advance of the left side. The rider, therefore, should position his right seatbone slightly in front of his left to accord with the horse's body. His right hip is similarly in advance of his left hip, therefore, and his right shoulder equally in advance of his left shoulder. The body is carried straight, not twisted, with the shoulders of the rider directly over the

hips. Again, the forward-and-down action of the small of the back absorbs the movement so that the seatbones stay in contact with the deepest part of the saddle and do not bump up and down, which is extremely uncomfortable for both horse and rider.

Turns, Circles and Changes of Direction

It is impossible to ride as is so often taught, with the rider's shoulders parallel to the horse's shoulders and the hips parallel to the horse's hips, without the rider's body being twisted. On an arc (circle, turn or bend) at walk or trot, the rider should imagine a line drawn through the horse's shoulders to the centre of the circle as forming one line of radius, a similar line drawn through the horse's hips as forming another radius, and one drawn through the rider's body

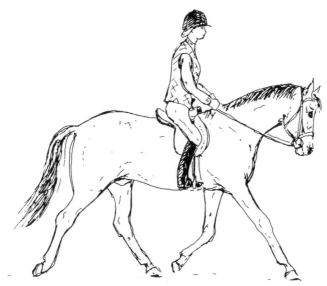

Fig 14   The correct position for rising trot with the rider's body slightly in front of the vertical.

*Fig 15   Horse and rider in right canter. The right side of
the horse's back is slightly in advance of the left side; therefore,
the rider positions his or her right seatbone slightly in advance
of the left to accord with the position of the horse's body. The
rider's shoulders are directly above his or her hips with,
obviously, the right shoulder slightly in advance of the left
shoulder. The rider is, therefore, in harmony with the horse.*

as forming a third radius between the
other two.

In canter, with, for example, the off
fore leading, because of the positioning
explained in the previous section, the
rider's body is turned slightly to the
outside of the circle (to the left). It should
not be turned in 'following' the circle as is
so often taught, as then the rider's body
would, literally, be at cross purposes with
that of the horse. The head, however,
must be able to move independently of
the body (a point well understood by any
trained dancer) and is turned in the

direction of the turn or circle.

When changing direction, weight is
transferred to the appropriate seatbone so
that the horse will naturally move in that
direction to maintain its own balance,
that is, weight on right seatbone to move
right.

In addition to weighting the seatbone,
at walk and trot the rider's body is turned
in the direction he wishes to go, again, so
that the horse will follow naturally. For
example, when executing a circle to the
left at walk or trot, the rider's body (on its
own radius) will be following the

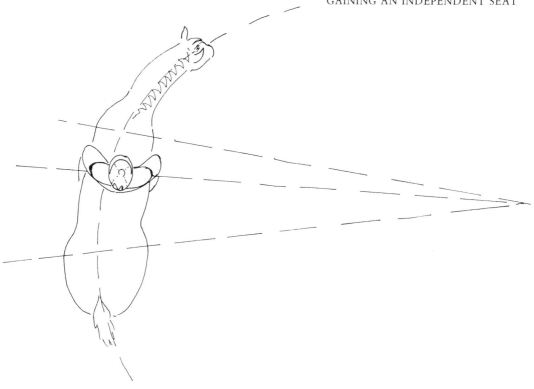

Fig 16   On an arc in walk or trot the horse's shoulders form one line of radius to the centre of the circle, the rider's body forms a second and the horse's hips form a third. (In canter, the position explained in Fig 15 is adopted, and the rider's head looks in the direction of the circle or turn.)

direction of the circle.

This weighting of the seatbones is also used for flying changes in advanced work. Because so many dressage riders do not seem to know about the correct positioning of the body in canter, we often see mechanical changes of leg obtained by forceful hands and legs with the body being thrown from side to side and 'kinking' at the waist, all of which is extremely ugly and detrimental to the horse. A change of leg obtained simply by a change in the position of the seatbones, however, is beautiful to see.

If a rider sits and moves correctly in this classical position, he will notice how his hands and legs remain stable, moving only when necessary, and the horse will carry him with ease and comfort. I have often seen people who sit on a horse with a body like a block of concrete, with only their legs and hands working, and the horse is more disturbed than helped by this way of riding.

The rider's most important aid is his body, including his weight distribution, and the most important contact point is the seatbones, which are positioned in the deepest point of the saddle and are vital in maintaining the horse's rhythm and cadence. They go with the movements of the horse's back in each pace.

The Hands

The upper arm should fall naturally down from the shoulder, down the side of the chest, with the elbow resting at the hip. The elbow should *not* be held in front of the hip as is often taught, as this creates a tendency to pull back on the rein, and is a serious fault.

The hands ask by rotating the wrists outwards so that the fingernails are uppermost and, through a gentle play on the reins with the fingers only, sending little signals or vibrations down the rein. A trained horse will not need more than an ounce or two of contact. Open rein is used for novice horses, decreasing as training progresses.

To slow down or stop, there is a slight taking in of the reins with the fingers only, nails uppermost, and a slight erecting of the body and bracing of the back (slight pushing forward of the seat).

The hands are used, from their base position above the pommel, laterally and vertically but never backwards. Once a rein aid has been complied with, the hands are immediately lowered again to say 'thank you' to the horse. This is not a signal for the horse to stop the movement; a trained horse continues the movement until you ask for something else or stop him. This is the technique known as *descente de mains* in classical equitation.

The Legs

The legs are held loosely and without tension down the horse's sides. Grip of any kind has no place in classical equitation. When the legs are used to reinforce the body aids, they are used in a stroking

Fig 17 *This drawing has been taken from a photograph (with likeness and clothing disguised) of one of the world's greatest classical riders. His correct classical position enables the horse to go peacefully and willingly in self carriage and in complete harmony with his rider.*

action, not a pinching one, from just behind the girth forward.

It is essential that the thighs are consciously open and loose and that there is no muscular tension in the legs or bottom. Otherwise, the rider cannot develop the feel through the seat on which this method of equitation is entirely based. The weight must fall naturally down through the heel which must never be consciously pushed down, nor the toes up.

Common Errors

The main error concerning the seat is that the rider is not sitting in the deepest part of the saddle. Very often, he will be too

Fig 18   Compare this picture with Fig. 17. It has been drawn (again with the likeness disguised) from a photograph of one of Britain's top competitive dressage riders. Her body is twisted at cross purposes with that of her unfortunate horse. Her hands are harsh and pulling as she tries to cope with her horse's inevitable resistance and difficulty in coping with the rider's completely unclassical position – her shoulders are too far forward, her seat too far back and the whole presents a thoroughly tortuous picture.

far back, where the horse finds it difficult to carry him due to its own conformation and natural balance. The rider often wrongly sits too close to the loins where the shape of the horse's body is more rounded, and it is difficult and uncomfortable for him to sit. The second main error is the twisting of the body caused by faulty instruction to the rider, on a circle, to 'put your shoulders parallel to the shoulders of the horse and your hips parallel to the hips of the horse'. This has three bad consequences.

The first is that the body is twisted during the circle and cannot be used properly to accompany the movement of the horse's back, keeping the cadence and the impulsion. Secondly, by twisting the body to the inside of the circle, the weight of the rider is thrown to the outside, so increasing the bad effect of the centrifugal force instead of compensating for it. Thirdly, the inside leg, so important for the in-curving and support of the horse, is raised, it starts to grip and very often the inside stirrup is lost. What also often happens in this situation is that the rider is hanging on to the inside rein, which is the worst mistake possible for work on the circle.

Far too often we see arms which are rigid, and badly placed with the elbows in front of the hips, the weight of the arm throwing the shoulders forward and unbalancing the body by making it also tip forward. A bad position of the head causes similar effects. A bad carriage of the rider's head is when the head is tipped to one side or another, causing a consequent collapsing of the hips on the same side, thus shifting the weight and cancelling the use of the back, as a twisted back cannot work correctly. If the head is 'dropped' forward, it will bring the shoulders forward, shift the seat back and upset the whole balance and efficiency of the rider.

Nodding the head, particularly common in trot and sometimes even in walk, not only looks ridiculous but also does nothing to help the rider's all-important balance and stillness of the shoulders. If the shoulders are moving the hands probably are, too.

You must not have your shoulders moving and your back rigid – this is, in fact, totally opposite to the correct method. The shoulders and head must be immobile and the back supple. If your back is supple and absorbs the movement of the horse in the way previously described, you are able to keep your shoulders still. With a rigid, stiff back you will always have rigid, stiff shoulders, resulting in similarly rigid and stiff arms which cause unsteady hands and harsh use of the bit.

Errors concerning the legs are rigidity and unsteadiness, disturbing the horse often to the point where he either 'goes on strike' and refuses to work, or charges away, which is another form of revolt. I have seen many students in trouble from a terrible and very common squeezing of the leg. This upsets many horses, whereas others become unresponsive to the leg aid.

Master Oliveira maintains that the most important part of the position is not that of the top of the back but that from the middle of the back to the knee. He also says, 'I want to see on a horse a rider with a relaxed body and legs without muscles!' One of my students once brought me a video taken during a course with an expensive overseas dressage instructor. I was horrified to hear him say repeatedly, 'When you use your leg I should almost hear the horse's bones cracking'. This is absolutely contrary to all the principles of classical equitation.

It is particularly rare to see riders carrying their hands properly, except perhaps in Portugal. I so often see knuckles facing each other and turning towards the stomach of the rider and, in doing so, pulling more and more. The hands should be carried vertically and their movement should always be lateral or vertical. As a rule, the inside hand in-curves and invites, and the outside

hand gives, supports, collects and slows the horse.

Riders practising the above errors 'destroy' their horses and accuse them of all sorts of faults and vices that they do not have. Those horses are simply much too sensitive for such rough-and-tumble riders.

Acquiring a Secure, Independent Seat

The most useful exercise which enables the student to feel the back of the horse moving underneath him, and which also develops the rider's use of his back, is the sitting trot on the lunge. Before a lesson, the instructor must explain to the student the mechanics of each of the horse's gaits and the correct positioning and movement of the rider's body for each gait, as detailed earlier in this chapter.

As most lunge work is done on a circle, the instructor should also explain to the student the effects of a force that is barely mentioned yet is encountered on every circle – the centrifugal force. On a large circle at walk the force will be minimal but on a small circle at canter it will be much greater, and the tendency is for the rider to be carried towards the outside of the circle. However, by sitting in the correct, classical position so that the rider is with the horse rather than against him, and by weighting the inside seatbone and allowing more weight to travel down the inside leg, the effects of the centrifugal force will be considerably lessened.

As the student learns to feel through his seat what is happening underneath him, with no stirrups or reins, he will soon develop feelings of balance, confidence and safety as he discovers he no longer has to grip to stay with his horse, but maintains his position by means of balance and relaxation.

To be able to feel the movements of the horse's back, there must be no tensing of the muscles of the buttocks, which should remain quite relaxed, and the rider should pretend he has no use in his legs. They should drop comfortably and naturally along the sides of the horse and the toe must fall naturally *downwards* (as in *voltige*), not up as is usually taught. If the toes are up, they can only be kept there by means of muscular contraction. Muscles can work only by contracting; they cannot stretch themselves as is often supposed. If the leg muscles are contracted there is an inevitable muscular tension and rigidity which blocks the feel of the horse's back and limb movements through the seat and so prevents the rider accompanying those movements and developing the essential balance.

As the rider becomes used to having 'useless' legs and a totally relaxed bottom with loose, open thighs, he should be asked to tell the instructor, without looking, which hind leg is moving forward when. He should be asked to close his eyes and, by feeling the alternate hollowing or dipping of each side of the horse's back through his seat, call out 'left, right, left, right . . .' After a time, the rider should be able to call out correctly each time, on request. At that point, he will have gained the basic elements of feel so essential to harmonious, classical equitation, and, by constant practice, will be able to carry it through when riding off the lunge.

It is important, when riding with stirrups, to remind yourself not to use them to brace or fix the legs. They should simply take the weight of the ball of the foot. The seat and legs remain open, loose and relaxed, the leg simply brushing from front to back when a leg aid is needed. As soon as there is any gripping, the feeling of the horse's back through the seat will disappear altogether and balance and harmony will be lost.

Conclusion

I have so far mentioned the tuition of Master Nuno Oliveira, who is without doubt the master rider of this century and whose teachings are those of the great French rider, de la Guérinière. I want now to mention also a great German master, Steinbrecht, a nineteenth century rider.

I am very opposed to present-day German-style dressage riding, but it has not always been so heavy, rigid, dictatorial and ugly as it is now. Until the beginning of the twentieth century, German riding was brilliant – it was extremely refined as well as technically excellent. Steinbrecht's book, the translated title of which is *The Gymnastics of the Horse*, is a real bible for any rider who wants to reach a good level of equitation. His opinions concerning the position on the horse coincide very much with the technique and tuition of Master Nuno Oliveira:

There is unfortunately a very strong idea rooted in so many people that one should have one position, let us call it 'normal' position, for everything. Unfortunately, this leads towards a mechanisation of the rider and discourages and sends away many young riders who prefer to go directly into hunting, racing or jumping, where they feel they have more freedom.

39

The normal position, meaning a position which will be convenient for the majority of cases, does not exist. The rider is only positioned on a horse properly when the vertical of the centre of gravity of his body and the vertical of the centre of gravity of the horse are on the same line. In such a way, the rider and the horse are one. It is called in French 'centaurisation'. The position of the rider must be shifting permanently, to accord with the moving centre of gravity of the horse. The rider must adapt his position each time.

For twenty years I flew all sorts of aircraft. During a flight, the centre of gravity of an aircraft changes constantly. It is the pilot's job to correct and adapt the position of the aircraft in such a way that the aircraft is put back in balance and flies all by itself, as it were. In this respect, there is a great similarity between flying and riding.

I feel those who dispute this explanation have never trained a horse, have never felt underneath them a light, self-carrying horse who responds to and obeys the slightest aid given through the weight of a rider properly trained, who knows how to use his body.

To obtain this proper use of the body and feel the different positions required by the horse in different movements, Steinbrecht explains how, in olden times, the old masters put their students on perfectly trained horses, with no stirrups or reins, between the pillars or on the lunge so they learned with ease and felt how the horse was moving, and learned how to move with him. Today, exactly the same principles are taught and applied by the French masters and Master Oliveira.

Steinbrecht deplored the fact that this form of tuition could not be given in the military cavalry and also said that this was the reason why it was almost impossible to train a horse or rider any more. Unfortunately, since that time a century ago, riding instruction has, until very recently, been almost entirely in the hands of the military.

General l'Hotte, a great French rider, was well aware of the situation and tried to correct this poor state of affairs. He said in his book *Equestrian Questions* that there are four different levels of riding. The first and highest is High School (classical riding), the second is *équitation extérieure* (outside riding) such as eventing, the third is racing and the fourth military riding. It takes some courage and honesty for a cavalry officer to establish this classification.

I shall finish with two recommendations from Steinbrecht. The first is about how to sit on a horse. So often teachers have enormous problems in sitting students vertically on a horse. Your spine and the spine of the horse in classical riding must always be at a 90-degree angle. This is the best way to be efficient with your back in the same way as the sun's rays are at peak efficiency when they are at right angles with the earth at noon on the equator.

The second recommendation is how, on the lunge, the student should be positioned properly with his leg totally relaxed and extended as much as possible, with no stiffness and with the toe pointing *down naturally*. A stiff leg and raised toe leads to rigidity, and rigidity is the greatest enemy of quality equitation.

With all my heart, I ask every rider – young and not so young, male and female: have an honest try to position

*Fig 19   In classical equitation, your spine and the spine of
the horse must always be at a 90° angle. This is the best way to
ensure peak efficiency of your seat.*

yourself better. One day you will have the reward of the feeling of a horse who gives you his back, a deep and relaxed sensation, something beautiful, a great quality of life – and the happiness of being totally *with* your horse.

5 The Hands in Riding

by Charles Harris, FIH, FABRS, FBHS

Approximately 80 per cent of all riders have little or no idea of what constitutes the correct use of the hands when in the saddle, about 19.9 per cent have only a vague idea, and only around 0.1 per cent endeavour to use their hands correctly in general riding. Before discussing the efficient and correct use of the hands for

Fig 20 The author of this chapter giving the rider an introduction to the 'ABC' of the mechanics of the rider's hands.

general riding let me briefly outline what appears to be accepted as the normal use of the hands when riding:

1. Incorrect use of the hands when steering/guiding the horse.
2. Incorrect application of the hands trying to aid equine locomotion.
3. Incorrect application of the hands as an aid to maintaining rider balance when in the saddle.
4. Incorrect application of the hands to maintain body posture in the saddle.
5. Incorrect application of the hands as a substitute for the correct use of the legs.
6. Incorrect application of the hands as a means to support the seat and use of braced back.

Any one, or a combination of the above, severely limits the scope and correct use of the hands in riding, and in my humble opinion is greatly to blame – the world over – for poor riding standards and so many riding accidents.

Some Essential Requirements

What should be borne in mind by all riders and riding teachers is that there are some basic requirements which, without careful consideration, will limit the progress of riders who wish to use their hands correctly to enhance the quality of their riding.

1. It is essential when horse and rider meet, that they should be on good terms with each other – and in the case of a problem horse, on the best possible terms.
2. Although the rider might well be able to apply the correct techniques, it is still possible not to give the horse the confidence and communication intended.
3. No two human beings are alike, no two horses are alike, no two days are alike, and no two rides/lessons are alike, therefore there are no 'identical repetitive aid patterns' which, once learnt by the rider, are applicable to every horse.
4. The rider's hands are used in many activities daily, and it is these same hands which come into play when using the reins. So good hands are a matter of conscious thought and daily practice.
5. Good hands can, and should, be taught to all riders. Valuable lessons on the correct feel and use of the reins can be given to the rider prior to mounting the horse.
6. A horse should not be considered as a physical mass to be shaped, or outlined to a standard mould. They do possess a nervous system and a brain. These are the primary means of getting the rider's message through, and in turn lead to suppleness, lightness, and efficiency.
7. The normal and hesitant gaps between thought and application of the hand aids must be eliminated if the rider wishes to obtain definite and correct responses from the horse.
8. The better the seat, posture, balance and position of the rider, the better will the rider be able to give clear and concise aids with the hands. Extremely active 'busy' hands with the so-called, overdone 'give and take' nonsense – with hands and fingers going 'fifty to the dozen' – will leave the horse mentally and physically confused.

Fig 21   The lightness and ease of the horse and the bit in the
travers haunches-in at the trot.

Definition of Good Hands

Good riding hands are those which know when and how to act on the reins with the correct minimum tension and contact to convey clearly to the horse the educated intentions of the rider, which the horse readily accepts and obeys.

Good hands cannot exist without the full use and support of all the other bodily functions of the rider – anatomically, physiologically, and psychologically. To this end riders should be given some elementary knowledge in horse and rider physics and mechanics.

It is my firm belief – proved in practice time and time again – that the correct use of the hands in horse riding can be taught and learned. Looked upon at first as a science, with thoughtful experience it can develop into an art form, furthering equestrian achievement, pleasure, and riding safety.

The Music of the Hands

Let me briefly describe what the actions of my hands are when seated in the saddle. I try to mount every horse – including problem horses – as quickly and smoothly as possible, and when seated in the saddle endeavour to sit 'light and still'. With the minimum of fuss I adjust my reins so both have a similar contact on each side of the horse's mouth, although this does not necessarily mean a consistent contact on the two bars, and lips of the horse. Then, with an almost imperceptible and extremely slow side-to-side movement, I try to obtain a gentle, soft easing of the horse's lower jaw. These reactions to the reins I call 'music'.

Obviously the weight contact with the mouth varies from horse to horse, and with gait, figure, and direction, with the aim being to use the minimum of tension. This imperceptible activity is going on all the time – no matter what else I may be doing with the reins in my hands, this gentle to-and-fro on the reins keeps me in full conversation and communication with the horse's behaviour and intentions. These hand actions are fully supported by legs, seat, weight, and balance.

In effect, each hand carries out more than one task, inviting the horse to comply in the desired manner. There is a continuing interplay with both hands through the reins to the horse's mouth, helping to calm, position, and place it in the correct mental and physical attitude so that it finds it easier to comply than evade or resist the hands. This is much the same as the way in which a good pianist develops musical talent based on correct finger and scale exercises. In both cases, correct use of the hands originates in good body posture.

Functions of the Hands in Riding

Count Eugenio Martinengo Cesaresco, whose works on scientific horsemanship raised many an eyebrow in Europe during the second half of the last century, goes a long way to summing up the range and importance of the hands in riding:

1. To form the mouth of the horse – that is, to teach it to obey the aids of the hands, which are our orders.
2. To place and keep it in such a

position that it is mechanically obliged to obey the orders of the hands.

3. To make it assume the various preparatory positions, in order to execute the desired evolutions.

4. To collect, and hold it collected, so as to cause it to execute given evolutions, and prevent its putting itself in those attitudes in which it can act against the rider.

5. To feel the movements of the horse, and through them to understand its intentions in order to impede their execution.

6. To distract it from these, and hold it attentive to us.

7. To keep it from falling, not materially, which is impossible, but preventatively – that is, to hold it in that position in which it is less liable to fall.

Looking first at point 1, the physiological structure of the horse's mouth must be brought into a state of readiness in which it can accept and be communicated with through the hands, reins and bit. This is brought about by encouraging the salivary (parotid) glands to remain soft and supple, thereby producing the saliva which acts as a lubrication to the bit lying across the bars of the horse's

Fig 22 *The subtlety of the rider's hand on the horse and the bit in a moment of canter pirouette.*

mouth. This to me is the preparation of the horse's mouth. Without this continuing lubrication, known as 'a wet mouth', the bit would be abrasive, rubbing on and damaging the tissues covering the bars of the lower jaw and the lips, resulting in a hot, hard, painful and dry mouth.

To teach the horse hand aids, the first stage is to get the horse to accept a light contact, a light feel on both reins; then a slow, light, imperceptible sideways feel on one or both reins in the same direction; then finally to bring into play any other rein effect the rider desires. A rider having good hands uses them to produce many varied effects – often at one and the same time – to improve the horse's overall efficiency and condition.

Point 2 concerns an important part of correct training. The horse first learns to move forward looking in the direction of movement on straight lines, circles and arcs. At this stage, the longitudinal line or curve of the horse is 'directed' from the front, that is its mouth, with the rest of its body following in the same line or curve. These figures make the least demand on the rider's hands.

Fig 23 *In every aspect of classical horsemanship the rider's/ trainer's hands must be inviting and truly musical to enhance the qualities of the horse and the bit.*

The horse is then taught to move sideways and forwards at the same time, looking in or away from the direction of movement, according to the rider's preference. It is by these carefully carried out gymnastic exercises, which teach the rider a range of hand aids with the minimum of tension, that the horse is encouraged, and invited, to move in the correct position, posture, angle and gait.

Because a horse is not a mechanical machine there are two ways which will lead or invite it to carry out various exercises correctly, as suggested in point 3. The first is the correct stage-by-stage positioning, and the second is the tempo or speed which permits the former to be carried out in a balanced manner.

It is only at the more advanced stages of correct training under the rider that the horse is able to use itself in the fully collected manner mentioned in point 4. What is essential from the start, is that the horse moves and uses itself in a *united* manner, something very different from the 'shortened form and outline' and 'gaits' of true collection.

The main absorption of equine movement is through the rider's lumbar region, seat, and thighs. The hands and legs ensure that the horse's movement is harmonic, according to his stage of training. Used correctly, the hands act as a finely-tuned gauge to check and assist the mental and physical condition of the horse. For example, once its lower jaw tightens or stiffens, or becomes in any way rigid, it immediately has an adverse effect on the going and behaviour of the horse.

To correctly fulfil the requirement of Cesaresco's final point is to keep the horse upright and supple, that is, with its four limbs and body vertical to the ground. Any leaning or tilting to the right or left immediately affects speed and balance and the correct use of the horse's limbs in all general purpose riding.

The rider's hands are an important aid to the processing of the horse's mental and physical qualities by controlling what should be the most sensitive part of the horse's body – the inside of his mouth.

... A good rider has a thinking mind, fine emotions, and a sensitive hand ...
Tu Yu, 72 BC

6 Snaffles and Gags

by Dorothy Johnson, FBHS

Sitting on the back of a horse, riding it and controlling it may seem a perfectly normal, everyday happening. But when you look at this objectively it is quite amazing that a huge, naturally shy animal like a horse allows man, often in the form of a lightweight young girl, to sit on it, encircle it with a pair of legs and guide and regulate its paces by means of a piece of metal held in its mouth – the bit.

Plain Jointed Snaffle

The bit most in use the world over and for many years past is the snaffle, and it is to be found in various forms, the most useful being the plain jointed snaffle. It must be obvious that the control of this big animal does not come from the bit alone – whatever kind of bit it may be. For behind every bit is a pair of hands and behind every pair of hands is a pair of legs. The brain of the rider is trained by experience and instruction until it has the requisite knowledge to receive from the horse indications of its behaviour. This educated brain then makes the rider's legs, hands and body co-ordinate properly to pass back to the horse the required signals needed to control him.

Some of these signals or aids come down the reins to the bit. All knowledgeable trainers will start with the snaffle. It used to be normal practice to use a mouthing bit (a snaffle, or often a straight bar snaffle with keys dangling from it), so that the horse rolled them about with his tongue, making a nice wet mouth. Now thinking is different; too much of this playing with the bit makes the horse put its tongue in the wrong place – too far back, or even over the bit. Also, these bits were often too wide or the wrong size and clumsy to use.

Most horses start work in a plain jointed snaffle. To me, such a bit is much easier for the horse, making it much clearer when asking for a sideways bend from the poll (lateral flexion), and allowing more space for the tongue.

Position of the Bit

Looking at the horse's mouth carefully, it is easy to see that the corners of the lips curve round over the bars of the mouth. (The bars are the space between the teeth where the bit lies.) Thus, when the reins are felt, the bit presses on the lips covering the bars in the corners of the mouth. Meanwhile, the joint allows the two sections of the mouthpiece to form a sort of triangle, a bit like a roof-top, which leaves plenty of room for the tongue to lie.

The straight bar snaffle, without a joint, (which many riders think is less severe because of the lack of joint, which in many minds conjures up thoughts of a

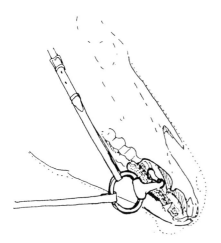

Fig 24 *With a jointed snaffle, the joint allows the two sections of the mouth-piece to form a triangle which leaves room for the tongue to lie.*

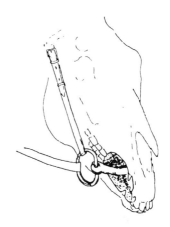

Fig 25 *A straight bar or mullen/half-moon mouthpiece lies flat across the mouth resting on the bars at either side and cushioned by the tongue in the centre.*

pinching nutcracker action) presses much more on the tongue. It lies flat across the mouth, resting on the bars at either side and cushioned by the tongue in the centre. I think pressure on the lips is much better tolerated by the horse than pressure on the bars. Decreasing the pressure on the tongue reduces the likelihood of the tongue coming over the bit.

When the horse is moving forward with the head and neck stretched forward and down and the rider's legs are closed, if contact is put on the reins the bit will move up into the corners of the mouth and cause the horse to raise its head. In simple terms, it does this to avoid the pressure. If contact on the rein is continued, and the legs are also used, the joint of the bit will begin to close and the horse, in response, will either slow down or become more gathered together – in the trained horse, this is a move towards collection. Again, if the rider and horse are trained, and the rider continues to ask, the horse will become submissive, that is

a flexion will be offered.

It may help to clarify the action of the bit in your mind if you think of the position of the horse's head in relation to your hand. When the head is low and the hand higher, the bit moves up, but as the head comes level with the hand, the bit stays steady.

The place where the bit should lie in the mouth will vary slightly. On the whole I think riders fit the snaffle too low. They are thinking about just wrinkling the corners of the mouth, and forget that because of the joint, the bit is dangling down much too near the front teeth! It is a good idea to put the first finger and thumb of each hand near the ring and straighten the mouthpiece, to help to fit it up to the corners. The lower the bit the more severe it becomes. If there is a tongue problem then it needs to be as high as is necessary to discourage this. I very rarely need to lengthen the fitting of the snaffle, but I often need to raise the bit.

Choosing a Bit

There is a wonderful saying, 'there is a key to every horse's mouth', which is often taken to mean that if we find the bit to suit the horse, all will be well. But if you watch the best trainers of horses, those who have time and patience, those who want to produce the genuine article, not those who for business reasons have to do a quick job, you will see that they all ride in normal snaffles. However much we may yearn to ride as well as these top trainers, many of us fall short of this standard, and so we may find that we need a bit of help in the form of a different bit to enable us to get a similar result. So perhaps the key is not to the horse's mouth but to our riding knowledge and ability.

You will note that I have not used the word hands, but rather riding knowledge and ability. The words hands is in my way of thinking a shorthand term covering good legs, a supple and therefore still position, which enables the rider to move or maintain the hand contact, and the experience and feel to use this correctly and at the right time.

As a teacher I am lucky enough to be involved with many riders keen to train their horses correctly. Often they need to change the type of snaffle to help them to get through their difficulties; then when the problem is overcome they can return to the normal bit.

On the principle that a piece of wire cuts cheese, a thin mouthpiece is more severe than a thick one. But common sense must prevail, and well-bred horses with little mouths are very uncomfortable in great thick bits. Some of these thick bits are very heavy too.

Horses vary in temperament – there are light horses which rather prefer to sit back behind the rider's hand, and there are others which are always wanting to be one pace faster than required. If your horse is one of the former then he will be more willing to draw forward into a genuine contact if he has a normal mouthpiece than if he has a thin one. But the second type might be easier for an amateur to ride with a thinner mouthpiece. Horses will also vary in conformation, having light, well raised front ends, or strong heavy shoulders.

Those who ride well will find the type of snaffle in which their horse goes forward and, of course, slows down when required, and they will progress with the animal's training until it is ready to work in a double bridle. The double bridle should not, however, be used all the time – even Grand Prix horses work in snaffles some of the time. The double bridle consists of a bridoon – a smaller version of a snaffle – and a curb bit so that most of the directions come down the bridoon (snaffle) rein and the curb is used when extra submission is needed.

However, those who may not be so capable may find that they are able to exert their authority over their horse more easily if they change to a thinner snaffle for a few days, then change back to the thicker bit. On the other hand if they have been overdoing things, perhaps restricting the length of stride too much in their efforts to keep a rhythm, riding in the less demanding thicker bit may redress the fault.

Loose-Ring Snaffles

Metal snaffle bits are fashioned in stainless steel; nowadays, very few are to be found of nickel. The nickel ones are of a

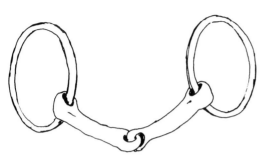

Fig 26   A plain, jointed, loose-ring snaffle.

yellowish tinge while the steel ones look a bluer colour. Avoid the nickel types as they are not strong enough and the metal, being soft, wears away at the points of movement. The joint in the centre of the mouthpiece wears away and becomes very thin, and in my youth, which was many years ago, I was caught out when the bit parted and I was left riding along with no bit in the horse's mouth! The other place where there is friction is at each side, where the rings pass through

Fig 27   'Most horses go well in a loose ring snaffle.'

Fig 28   Loose ring snaffles, particularly when they have large,
rounded rings like this, are often known as wire-ring snaffles.
Here is one on a 2-year-old Thoroughbred filly in preparation
for her first season's racing.

the end of the mouthpiece. The hole through which the ring goes becomes large and elongated, and the sides of the hole sharpen so that they may cut the lips in the corners. Although it may take many years before steel bits wear, some do become sharp, when they must be discarded. I have seen rubber bit guards, or 'biscuits' as they are sometimes called, used as a safeguard, but it is not good practice.

In spite of this drawback with loose ring snaffles, I do find most horses go well in them. If a horse is to accept the leg and move forward with powerful springing steps, swinging in its back and maintaining a light and lively contact on the rein, the bit in its mouth must be capable of elastic movement. The loose rings enhance this feel. The hand can persuade with the smallest indication because the mouthpiece can move that bit easier on the rings.

Fulmer Snaffles

Of course, as in all things there is the reverse side of the coin. Some horses have very frothy, chewing, mobile mouths. This is not necessarily due to a fault in their training, nor is it always because they are nervous and extra sensitive. But these horses may be better in a Fulmer-type snaffle. When Robert Hall returned to his school in Fulmer after his training at the Spanish Riding School, he started to use these bits and they became known as Fulmer snaffles. They have a full cheek at each side and the top of the upper cheek slots into a loop which has been attached to the cheek strap of the bridle. This keeps the mouthpiece very still and ensures that the flatter part of it is always lying against the mouth. If the cheeks are

not slotted into the loops, then the mouthpiece turns over and the narrower part is in contact, making it more severe. It does help when riding a horse with an over-mobile mouth; it may also help with a rider who finds difficulty in keeping a consistent contact. Perhaps the horse may be difficult to sit on, not the smoothest of rides, and the rider may be making it more difficult by losing the contact and taking it up again with a bit of a jerk. This is a kind of chicken-and-egg situation which is a common occurrence in horse riding!

The Fulmer will never pull through the horse's mouth and because of this it has been used to help to turn horses which may be stiff one way; perhaps they are a bit nappy, or just falling out through the shoulder. As the rider begins to turn better, he may feel more confident, and can then get to the root of the problem and train the horse. Unfortunately, the Fulmer can also make some horses more difficult to turn. The large cheek lying up the outside of the face is quite a comfortable thing to lean on and some animals

Fig 29   A Fulmer snaffle with its upper cheeks properly slotted into the keepers on the bridle cheekpieces.

do just this, so they are better with a loose ring or eggbutt type.

Of course, the bit itself does not resolve the problem of the difficulty in turning, as that is due to lack of training – the horse is stiff and finds it difficult to bend. As with humans, when a job is difficult and requires effort, we make excuses not to do it; the horse does the same and we call it napping or we say the horse is stupid. Most of the time the horse is either rather brighter than others, or it is confused. It is our fault, in failing to train it properly – either we have not made it equally supple on each side, or we are not being consistent and clear with our aids. These bits will help us to sort out the difficulty, but the knowledge and expertise of the trainer really produces the result.

Eggbutts and Rubber Snaffles

The eggbutt snaffle is the most widely used of all snaffle bits. I asked a young rider the other day why she used this bit, and she told me it was because it looked nice! However, there are other obvious advantages: in the main, the rounded end of the mouthpiece tapering to the ring, above and below the bit, makes sure that there is not a sharp edge to catch the lips. This egg-like join gives the bit its name. It is less mobile than the loose ring and so the mouthpiece is a little more still. Any loss of mobility is offset by the smoothness of the ring join, that is the eggbutt. I think it is important not to go overboard for the roundness of the eggbutt, because I have seen the sides of horses' cheeks bruised, rubbed, and with the skin broken.

These injuries have been due to a fat and chunky join between the mouthpiece and bit ring, the kind that often seem to be

Fig 30   The eggbutt snaffle makes sure the corners of the horse's mouth cannot be pinched between mouthpiece and ring. Because the mouthpiece is less mobile than a loose or wire-ring snaffle, it is a little more still.

found with fairly thick rubber-covered or vulcanite jointed snaffles. I know that the rubber snaffle has its devotees, but I find it hard to join their ranks. Those who use them really believe that their horses go better in them and that it is not possible to ride successfully in a metal bit. The problem is not in the mouth, or very rarely so, it is that the horse has not been taught to understand and respond to the rider's leg. As the horse does not motivate itself, it does not move the shoulders freely and bend around the leg bringing the hind legs forward under the body and so swinging in the back, stretching the neck forward and down and accepting the contact of the bit. What happens is that the horse just runs forward in little quick steps with a stiff back, throwing its head up and probably opening its mouth. If the rider avoids this, being very quiet and light, and the horse has the rubber bit, it may give the impression that it is going well, but in fact, and very sadly, it is not moving in its natural way but trundling quietly along. Perhaps if the horse is very established in its way of going and its rider wishes to hack about the country-side enjoying the feel of riding on horse-back then both will be quite happy with the rubber bit. But I must have the last word and say that they don't know what they are missing – there is more to riding!

Racing Snaffles

I recently saw a photograph in a daily paper of the great racehorse Legal Bid. There he was, winning an important race, at Chester I think, with the snaffle pulled right out of the mouth and his jockey controlling him with the leather rein in the mouth. Yet he still won, what a horse! I noticed that when he ran in the Derby he was bitted in a D-ring snaffle. This, as its name implies, has rings in the shape of a letter D and the straight side is placed next to the lips, which helps to keep it square in the mouth. It is used a lot in racing circles and I have heard it referred to as a racing snaffle.

Some racing snaffles have a fairly thin mouthpiece and very large bit rings for the same reason. The Newmarket Snaffle has a cheek at either side, similar to the Fulmer, but the cheeks are not moulded on to the mouthpiece in the same way, and they are not fitted into the keepers on the cheekstraps. Similarly they are made in pony sizes and you may see many small children riding equally small ponies, scampering about the country-side, or playing gymkhana games, giving rather strong rein aids without much leg. Yet the ponies seem to oblige, and the bit stays in place.

Sizes

It is surprising how many well bred and pure bred horses, with small heads and neat little mouths, need to be fitted with bits normally sold as suitable for ponies. Riders nearly always have to return to their saddlers and change the bit for a less wide fitting, which makes me wonder if horses nowadays have smaller heads and narrower mouths. I am often saying to riders, in the course of training sessions, that I can see too much of the snaffle bit, which is pulled out to the side of the mouth. It is nearly always on the left side – the riders must have weak left legs! Often when we look at the bit it is too wide, which must be very uncomfortable for the horse, with the joint no longer central but almost on the lips on the left side, and no space for the tongue. I rarely see bits too narrow, perhaps because it is easier to see when the sides of the mouth are being pinched.

Multi-Jointed Snaffles

Some snaffles have more than one joint – the French snaffle and the Dr Bristol are made with a link in the centre, so that there are two joints, one either side of the link. The French snaffle has a rounded link which makes it less severe than the Dr Bristol which has an angled flat link or plate. When the mouthpiece is at a certain angle the edge of this plate comes in contact. As soon as a second joint is added to the mouthpiece, the roof-top space for the tongue is lost, and the tongue comes in for more pressure. Because there is more mobility in the mouthpiece, those horses which get rather set laterally at the poll, and tend to set one side of the mouth, do seem to be easier to keep more

57

flexible and light. However, those horses who have proportionally large or sensitive tongues are not as quiet in their mouths as one would wish. They overplay with the tongue, even to the extent of drawing it back and wanting to put it over the bit, or sometimes the reaction is to take too much of a hold.

I was trying to explain to a young rider that the more joints there are the more severe is the bit and I remembered that years ago when I first came to work for Harry Monks I was put up on a chestnut with a short tail, a Hackney called Planet, an open show jumper, and I was told that unless I rode him in the bridle with the chain snaffle I would not be seen again. The mouthpiece was rather like a large curb chain and the bit rings were fairly large either end. Obviously the chain snaffle is the most severe, and how many joints are there in the chain?

Hanging Snaffles

Some riders say that the D-ring snaffle puts some pressure, though very little, on the poll. I find it difficult to accept this, but no doubt those with a mathematical mind will have the exact answer. The hanging snaffle, that looks rather like the top part of a Pelham bit, and has a similar attachment to the cheek strap of the bridle, most certainly does exert some pressure on the poll. This bit will help the rider who may not be quite as strong in the leg and supple in the shoulders, whose horse tends towards tension and excitement which shows itself in a raising of the head. The hanging snaffle or snaffle with cheeks enables those riders to maintain a suppleness at the poll which eases the physical tension and likewise the excitement. The bad news is that you are

unable to compete under British Horse Society Dressage Rules in this snaffle. However, you may use a bridoon of this type with your double bridle.

Gag Bridles

The gag snaffle, by its very name, comes in for much abuse, and evokes shrieks of horror when mentioned to some. This is understandable, and in an ideal world of ideal riders it would never be needed. But if you have ever been sent out with a sporting Northern pack, mounted on a horse who has raced, and which needed to be qualified to run in this year's point-to-point races, you might, like me, be jolly glad you had the gag snaffle!

It should always have a direct rein to the ring of the bit, as well as the gag rein. The gag is from time to time misused. Those riders who may not have the time or inclination to polish their riding may be seen on really good honest and courageous horses, which are being over ridden and upset by flapping legs and an 'electric bottom' using the gag in an over-strong and cruel way. In fact, they are ruining a really good horse, which would

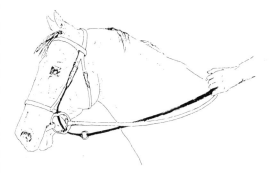

Fig 31 A gag snaffle correctly used, with two reins.

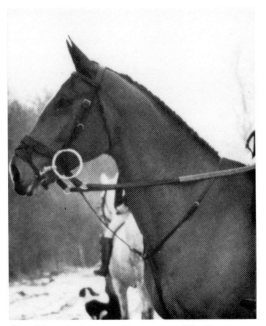

Fig 32   A cherry roller gag snaffle bit wrongly used with only one rein, with flash noseband and standing martingale.

not be pulling if it was well ridden. Having said all this, there is a place for the gag. Riders who are learning, who are not yet strong enough, often find that this bit helps them to stay at the right pace, without having to be so physically strong. This means that they can sit better and be more supple. They can use their legs without the horse running away, so the hocks come under, the paces improve, the jumping becomes less flat. After a period the gag can be dispensed with and a plain snaffle take its place.

The advantage of the gag action is that as the bit rises up the rounded rein towards the cheek straps it has the effect of raising the head, as opposed to letting the horse pull with its chin into its chest.

A group of riders were discussing types of bits and one was heard to say that she thought snaffles should be compulsory – maybe she was right.

Fig 33   The K.K. range of German bits. Top: Training Bit. A double jointed loose ring snaffle with egg link. Similar to a French snaffle but affording greater bearing surface and a comfortable, rounded link. Middle: Schooling bit. Eggbutt, port-mouthed snaffle with angled sides, so the risk of pinching the corners of the mouth is virtually non-existent. The port creates added bar pressure and, due to its being angled, discourages the horse putting his tongue over the bit. Bottom: Correction bit. A loose-ring ported snaffle allowing more bar pressure than a mullen mouth. Again, tongue evasion is discouraged with this bit.

7 The Double Bridle

by Anthony Crossley

Double bridles have been used, with varying degrees of intelligence or ignorance, as a means of improving a rider's control of his horse ever since they were first invented, in Naples, about the middle of the sixteenth century. During those 400 years, almost every imaginable and sometimes horrifying combination of bit has been tried, many of them being the direct cause of often prolonged torture to millions of horses throughout the so-called civilised world. High ports that scrape the roof of the mouth at a touch of the rein and spikes on the mouthpiece that cut into the gums are just two examples of the terrible things perpetrated in the name of horsemanship. Even today, many horses can be seen suffering quite severe discomfort or pain from ill-conceived or ill-used bits, and excessively high ports have been used in at least one popular display in Wembley within recent years. Any consequent disinclination of the horse to go forward towards the pain in his mouth was strongly discouraged by the positive application of very sharp spurs. The principle seems to have been that the horse must not run away but dare not stand still.

This sorry saga should not in any way be taken to imply that double bridles are in themselves evil things that should not be used at any time by right-minded people. It all depends on what the particular combination has been designed to achieve, and on whether the rider possesses the knowledge and the equestrian skill to use it correctly for that purpose and at all times. Intelligently and humanely designed and competently used, a double bridle can be a source of beauty and of considerable pleasure to both horse and rider. But if ignorance creeps into the design or the usage, the result is invariably shameful to the rider and more or less harmful and hurtful to the horse. It is therefore the duty of all horsemen to know what they are about when, and before, they use a double bridle.

A classic and simple example of the misuse of a double bridle arises all too frequently when a rider who does not know or understand the mechanical principles on which it is intended to operate just puts one into his horse's mouth on the assumption that it is merely a somewhat stronger bit than a snaffle, or perhaps because he thinks it is fashionable and looks good. The horse, also uneducated on the subject but full of high spirits, begins to go too fast and the rider pulls on both reins to check the speed. The two bits, perhaps incorrectly fitted and certainly incorrectly used, then begin to hurt the mouth; the horse inevitably tries to run away from the pain and so goes faster and faster and pulls harder and harder. As the rider pulls harder, the bit hurts more and more, and the horse's mouth together with its manners are on the way to ruination.

We ought to be able to do better than that, and so we can, if only we take the trouble. But it is astonishing, in view of the long history of horsemanship, how many riders still have little if any understanding of the technicalities of this potentially harmful tool called a double bridle – and it is always the horse who suffers.

Structure

The more eccentric or cruel combinations and contraptions that have been, and sometimes still are, put into the horse's mouth on the generally spurious assumption that there is somewhere a key to every horse's mouth other than the rider's hands, are best ignored. The simplest, most humane and, therefore, in the long run most effective form of double bridle comprises a snaffle, or bridoon, with a smooth mouthpiece, and one, or at most two, joints; and a curb bit, also with a smooth mouthpiece, a moderate port to ensure that the tongue is not compressed and a modest and well-proportioned cheek of which the lower portion will be 2–3in long and the upper portion not more than 1½in long. The fact that a thick mouthpiece is more gentle than a thin one in its contact with the bars of the mouth, for the curb bit as well as the snaffle, has to be weighed against the problem of not putting more bulk into the mouth than can be accommodated comfortably. Generally speaking it is best to err on the thick side rather than on the thin. It has to be remembered that the size of the incisor and molar teeth, at any rate in an adult horse, will ensure that there is always a substantial space between the upper and lower gums in which the bit or bits can lie.

The two bits must be sufficiently far apart to permit each of them to function efficiently without interference from the other, but without touching molars or tushes above or below them. But again, they must not be so far apart that there is a real risk of the horse putting its tongue between them and getting pinched. The joint of the bridoon will, of course, inevitably overlap the bar of the curb bit when the former hangs down from a loose rein.

Fallacious Theories

To have the bridle fitted correctly is only a beginning. It is even more important that the rider should know and understand the mechanical characteristics of the two bits, more especially the curb. Straight away we can dismiss the quite popular but simplistic and even fallacious idea that the bridoon operates to raise the horse's head and the curb to lower it, thereby implying that, armed with a double bridle, the rider is able to position his horse's head precisely where he wants it at any time. It may be true that the bridoon, which, after all, is nothing but an ordinary snaffle, can be used to raise the head, but it can also be used to lower it, as any dressage rider will know. And since the snaffle is usually used for the early stages of a horse's training, during which the very last thing we want to do is to raise the head by means of our hands and reins, we can perhaps agree that the snaffle has no special purpose beyond that of being a very practical and relatively humane all-purpose bit with no special refinements or abilities. Simple

Fig 34   A double bridle, showing loose ring bridoon and fixed-sided Weymouth.

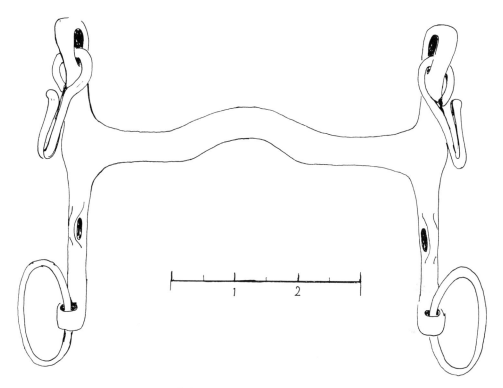

Fig 35   *A fixed-sided curb bit of the dimensions recommended by the author.*

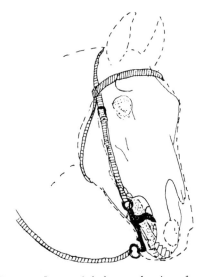

Fig 36   *In an adult horse, the size of the teeth ensures that there is sufficient space between upper and lower gums for the bits to lie.*

and straightforward in action, it can do little more than indicate to the horse the rider's wish to slow down or turn, since no rider however strong can force a horse to stop against its will. In the same way, no man can stop a bicycle, while remaining in the saddle, once the mechanical brakes have failed. Far more subtle means have to be devised and so, in both cases, it is best not to get into that situation in the first place. We may well conclude that the best use of a smooth and thick-mouthed snaffle is to encourage the horse to go forward with confidence, stepping boldly and without fear for its mouth, into the rider's hands.

If the bridoon has no refinements or niceties, the same cannot be said of the curb bit, though it certainly does not provide the rider with any direct and logical means of lowering the horse's head. Used with excessive force it might have the effect of pulling the horse's nose down or back until it reaches the chest, but that is not what it is designed to do and neither is it desirable that you should do that. Never try to pull the horse's head into any position of your own choosing, as this will inevitably be an unnatural position against which the horse will react with distress and aggression.

Broadly speaking, the purpose of the curb bit is, by means of its sophisticated action, to encourage the relaxation of the jaw. But the curb bit, just because it is armed with additional mechanical force through its leverage, can only be used to induce, but never to enforce, relaxation. Any form of force is the antithesis of relaxation.

The curb incorporates, by means of the curb chain behind the jaw, a greater or

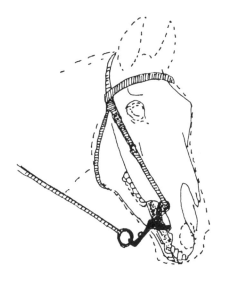

Fig 37 A diagram showing the lever effect of the curb bit and the fulcrum where the leather headstall is attached to the top of the metal cheekpiece of the bit.

lesser degree of lever action, depending on the length and relative proportions of the two parts of the cheekpiece, the fulcrum of the lever being the junction of the leather headstall with the top of the metal cheekpiece. The lever action comes into play each and every time the rein is taken up and the curb chain thereby tightened. This lever effect is a multi-plying force which means that a quite light pull on the reins by the rider will inevitably be felt by the horse as something very much stronger on its mouth, even though the rider is physically ignor-ant or unaware of the difference. Therein lies the danger. The indiscreet or ignorant rider will continue with his seemingly light contact and the horse will continue to endure a powerful, meaningless and compressing pressure on the bars of its mouth and tongue.

It should now be clear that the two parts of a double bridle exert quite diff-erent types or degrees of pressure on the horse's mouth and should, therefore, be handled quite differently through their respective reins – that is, the top or bridoon rein and the bottom or curb rein. But it is surprising how many riders appear to be under the impression that all they have to do is to grasp the two reins more or less indiscriminately with each hand, exerting a more or less indiscrimi-nate pull on both, and leaving it to the horse, without previous or further inst-ruction, to sort out the new and some-what intricate mechanical problems and react to them calmly, delicately and happily as to the manner born. Of course, nothing could be more absurd, and a much more intelligent approach is re-quired if any good results are to ensue.

The important point to note here is that the mechanically-boosted power of the curb bit should never be exerted permanently and without respite, as can be done without too much harm with the bridoon. If that is done, the horse, driven to distraction by a pressure that is too strong for it but which, because of the existence of the curb chain, it cannot escape, will either refuse to go forward properly or will learn to fight against the pressure with all the strength of the muscles of its neck and jaw. Fear and muscular habits die very hard, and it is likely that its mouth will be irretrievably ruined.

Tuition

First the rider must know exactly how the two parts of the double bridle, and more especially the curb bit, are intended to operate, separately or together. If he does not himself understand the technicalities he cannot expect the horse to find out. The horse has to be taught, so the rider must learn in order to be able to teach. If the horse does not understand and accept the reasons for a degree of mechanical or unnatural force being applied to its mouth, it will certainly resent it and endless trouble will result. So let us take one more, and in this case very detailed, look at the mechanical functions and justifications for the use of these two bits.

The Bridoon

The purpose of the bridoon is to restrain or steer the horse. In either case it can do no more than exert a simple and not excessive pressure on the mouth through the direct action of the rider's hands. If the bars of the bridoon are reasonably thick, and if the rider does not resort to any degree of wilful violence with his hands, the power of the hand action will not cause pain and will be many times less strong than the muscle power available to the horse in its neck and jaw. That imbalance of potential power in favour of the horse will be understood and appreciated by it, forming the basis of that confidence in itself and its rider that we seek from every horse and which, for better or worse, will make or mar his performance.

Provided the horse's head is carried, as a result of systematic training in a snaffle, in the more or less vertical position, as it should be for any bridle to be effective and certainly for all collected work, and notwithstanding the fact that the rider's hands are usually slightly higher than the horse's mouth, there will be virtually no tendency for the bridoon to slide up the lower jaw so that it rests and presses on the first molar. Its action will remain on the bars and the horse will work comfortably up to, or on to, the bit.

If, on the other hand, the horse, due to bad training, bad riding or bad manners, carries its head in a more or less horizontal position, the action of the bridoon will increasingly work up and back to the molars. This will stiffen the neck and back muscles, destroying the soft, lever action of the poll and with it the forward flow of impulsion from the quarters through the back and into the hand. So long as that flow is going through the horse, the snaffle will not of itself have any raising effect on the head, and the horse will be left to place its own head in accordance with its overall balance and degree of collection.

The simplicity and inherent gentleness of the bridoon, if properly used, enables

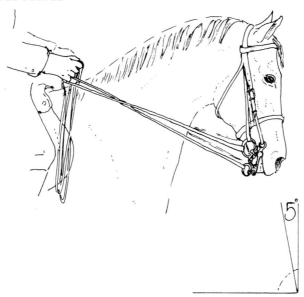

Fig 38   When the horse's head is carried more or less vertically, the action of the bridoon will remain on the bars and the horse will work comfortably up to, or on to, the bit.

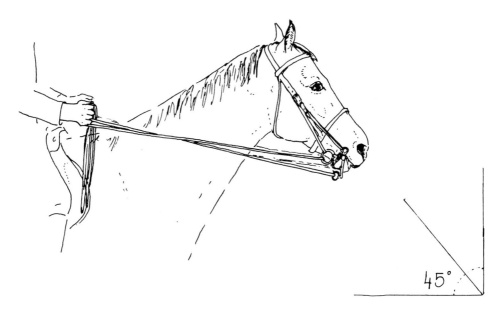

Fig 39   When the horse goes above the bit, the action of the bridoon will increasingly work up and back to the molars, stiffening the neck and back muscles, destroying poll flexion and the forward flow of impulsion from the quarters.

the rider confidently to maintain a consistent and steady contact with his horse's mouth at all times, and this in turn is a great assistance to the horse in maintaining its own balance.

The Curb

The purpose of the curb bit is not easy to define or describe. The conventional idea, usually lacking in precise explanation, is that it makes the horse lighter in hand and provides the rider with a more subtle means of control. It is generally acknowledged to be a far stronger bit than the snaffle because of its lever action, but just how that lever action works, or, indeed, just how the additional power is applied and for what purpose, is hardly understood by the majority of riders. It could be that the incompetently used curb bit acts, like the high port that scrapes the palate, to so frighten the horse that it will tend to put its head into a more or less fixed and vertical, or even overbent, position in which it can more easily evade the contact at the expense of going freely forward. That effect, as a 'worst situation', is absolutely possible, but it should not be accepted as the only one.

The essence of the curb bit theory lies in its mechanical application of greatly multiplied power resulting from its lever action. Power, in that context, means force. But we do not, or certainly should not, try to ride and control our horses by force. Perhaps the best we can say about this latent power is that the mere existence of its potential, quickly recognised by the horse, can be useful as a threat of ultimate sanction, though that is surely not a very convincing suggestion.

What do we expect the curb bit, with or without its full power, to achieve?

What exactly does it do? How does it help us? Clearly we do not expect to be able to stop a horse on which we are being carried along just by exerting an ever-increasing pressure on the bars of the mouth. Even if such pressure caused acute pain, it would still not stop the legs from propelling the horse forward. We must look elsewhere for a logical reason for using this powerful tool.

There are many forms of lever and this powerful and therefore dangerous one is comparatively complicated. A lever exerts its special power on its load when the following factors exist:

1. The lever (the cheek of the bit) is caused to revolve round a fixed fulcrum (the upper ring of the cheekpiece to which the curb chain and the headstall are attached). Virtually all power will be lost if the fulcrum is not effectively fixed by the correctly fitted curb chain. Without it, the lever will tend to revolve round its connection with the headstall, but the latter is not fixed and is, therefore, inefficient. There will also be some undesirable downward pressure from the headstall on to the poll.

2. The load (the point of contact of the bars of the bit on the bars of the mouth) is closer to the fulcrum than to the free or rein end of the lever (the length of the cheekpiece above the bar is shorter than the length below it). The greater the difference in those lengths, the greater the strength of the lever. It is worth noting that, in an equestrian context, the more equal the two parts of the cheek of a curb bit, the more gentle will be the effect in operation. And since it becomes extremely difficult to fit a curb chain properly with a very long upper cheekpiece, a bit that has a short upper cheek and a lower

cheek that is only 2–3in long will prove the most gentle. Ideally, neither section of the cheek should be long and the lower end should be only a little longer than the upper, certainly no more than three times as long.

3. If the fulcrum is fixed, and the contrasting lengths of the lever on either side of the load-point are satisfactory, great loads can be moved, or at least great pressure can be exerted on the point of load – that is on the point of contact of the bit on the bars of the mouth and tongue. But it can be taken for granted that no rider has even a remotely accurate idea of the degree of that pressure which he will have applied by the lightest touch on the curb rein but which he has no means of measuring. He will, in effect, be ignorant of what he is doing to his horse.

We may then ask whether there is anything good to be said for exerting any power or force, whether measured or unmeasured, on the horse's exceedingly sensitive mouth. The only thing we can be sure about is that it will cause pain to the very sensitive tongue and bars. It may be arguable that the threat of pain can be useful, but surely not the actual infliction of it.

In the midst of this tangle of conflicting arguments it is worth remembering that there can in the end be only one logical purpose for a curb bit, and that is to induce the horse to soften or relax his mouth. Even if we disregard any humanitarian factors, it seems unlikely that the infliction of pressure amounting to pain will produce that result. Everything that we know about horses tells us that they will go to great lengths to avoid or run away from pain because they are frightened of it. They are not stoical and will

not quietly put up with it. They will certainly not relax under its threat.

There is one other matter of overriding importance that must be considered. The fulcrum of the lever is the point of junction of the cheekpiece and the curb chain. The cheek and the chain are, therefore, from the point of view of action, inseparable. The lever or multiplying effect of one only acts by right of the existence of the other. The pressure of one is shared equally by the other. It follows that any downward or backward pressure of the bit will be equalled and counterbalanced by a forward or upward pressure by the chain on the chin groove. This means that there can be no purely backward pressure.

Using the curb rein with firmness therefore achieves nothing except to pinch the tongue and bars of the mouth between the nutcracker arms of the bit and the chain in a more or less painful manner that is beyond our powers of assessment. The only reaction we can reasonably expect from the horse to that unpleasant experience is either to close its teeth in rigid resistance to the discomfort or to withdraw its whole head in a vain effort to break the contact with the rein and the rider's hand, exactly as we would do to avoid the clumsy use of the drill by a dentist. These are not the reactions that we want.

Mise en Main Effect

All of this is surely more than enough evidence to make every thoughtful and humane horseman think very carefully before he decides to use a double bridle, and then to use it only in the most precise, delicate and calculating manner. And that manner, to comply with the normal principles of horsemanship, must exclude the use of force or the infliction of pain.

The only method of using the curb bit that follows these humane criteria is to use it for the sole purpose of creating or teaching a habit of relaxing the jaw as a reflex reaction to a light pressure on the tongue. If we can teach the horse to move its tongue, to lift it and then let it drop again under the bits, it will have relaxed the jaw and will start to salivate. This is the French *mise en main* effect, and it is invariably accompanied by a relaxation of the poll, the neck, the back and the joints of the hind legs. The invariable consequence of this is an improvement in balance, self-carriage and lightness.

With the double bridle, therefore, we use the bridoon to maintain a steady contact for the impulsion, and the curb to induce the repeated *mise en main* and with it lightness and better balance. They are two different and separate jobs, and no single bit could perform both satisfactorily. That is why, with all its problems and dangers, the good horseman will always use a double bridle for his advanced and polished work. Like all dedicated craftsmen, he needs good and often sophisticated tools, but he must himself acquire the knowledge and the skill to use them. In such circumstances, the curb rein will invariably be less taut than the bridoon rein.

Training the Horse

With these thoughts and principles in mind, the rider must now, quietly and patiently, set about the task of educating and instructing the horse in exactly what is expected of him in response to pressure

from the curb bit on the bars of his mouth. At first, you should work dismounted in the stable, and later mounted at a slow walk. Only when it is certain that the horse understands and will give the required response quietly and consistently, from the ground and when mounted at the walk, will it be safe to begin using the curb, little by little, at the trot and in other paces and movements. At this stage it is important to avoid any risk of the horse, through inattention or sudden loss of balance, blundering into a situation in which the curb bit is suddenly applied in a manner that is outside the control or intention of the rider. Such a situation would cause a degree of pain and fear that might take many months to overcome.

The first, in-stable stage of this teaching is to stand beside the horse's neck, facing the front, holding the bridoon reins with the right hand close behind the jaw, and the two curb reins with the left hand at a point about 9in from the metal cheek. At this point, and before thinking of anything else, always check that the curb chain is lying flat and untwisted in the chin groove and is short enough to prevent the bit from being pulled back to more than 35 degrees from the line of the jaw.

Give the horse a few minutes to feel the two bits in its mouth, and hopefully to lift and drop its tongue a few times to become aware of the amount of movement it can create, especially with the curb bit. Then begin the lesson by taking a firm contact with the bridoon reins and try to get the horse to carry its head within about five, or at most ten, degrees to the vertical. When you are satisfied that it is paying attention and standing quietly, gently take a light but steady contact with the

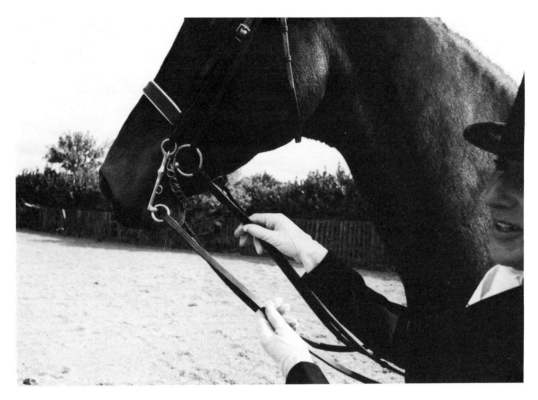

Fig 40   The trainer stands beside the bridled horse, facing forward, right hand holding the bridoon reins about 4in behind the jaws, left hand holding the curb reins about 9in from the lower ring, ready to exert backward pressure.

curb rein, watching and feeling very carefully for any reaction from the horse. The reaction we do not want is that it should show any sign of moving backwards. This is not a common reaction, but if it occurs the curb contact must be dropped immediately and the horse pushed forward again with the right hand.

The reaction that we hope for is a visible relaxation, or giving, of the lower jaw, preferably accompanied by a lifting and dropping of the tongue and without any parting of the lips. Be prepared to maintain the pressure on the bit for a few

moments if necessary, to give ample opportunity for the reaction to occur. Do not try to obtain it by force – if it does not occur within five or ten seconds, relax everything and start again. The horse will soon loosen and shift its jaw as a natural reaction to the persistent pressure on it. In all probability there will be a moment or two of mystified immobility of the jaw when you first exert the pressure, in which case you may increase it just a little though never to the point of brute force or of trying to hurt. A little patience, and perhaps a little give and take if there is prolonged immobility, will almost invariably produce the effect you want within a minute or so at the most, and the battle will have been won.

On the instant that you see or feel the horse move or relax his jaw, relax the curb pressure entirely and caress the horse and perhaps reward him with a titbit. Repeat the lesson three or four times, always rewarding the correct response, then remove the bridle and proceed with the day's work with a snaffle.

The immediacy of those first rewards is vital, and it is for that reason that the first lessons are given dismounted so that the teacher can use his eyes as well as his hand to sense the initial and all-important movement of the mouth. Horses are quick to learn and very quick to appreciate kindly reactions from their human controllers. It will only require a few daily repetitions of the co-operative sequence of bit pressure-mouth relaxation-reciprocal relaxation, for the lesson to be well absorbed. The horse will then become increasingly confident about the double bridle, and there will never be any excuse for that pulling and counter-pulling that so mars the performance of an ill-trained horse and rider. Never, that is, provided the rider does not forget and begin to abuse his power, thereby setting up reactionary resistance from the horse.

Fitting the Curb Chain

The curb chain must be set so that it lies perfectly smoothly from end to end. This will always be so if the following golden rule is followed. First fit the chain on to the offside hook so that, when twisted clockwise, the upper part of the link on the hook will be on the inside of the hook. Then, standing on the near side, twist the chain clockwise again until it is firm and flat along its inner length, holding the end in your left hand. Transfer the chain to your right hand, keeping your fingers on the inside, next to the horse's jaw, and your thumb on the outside of the last link.

The last link is then placed on the nearside hook *with your thumbnail uppermost*, without letting go of the chain and without altering the grip. Slide your hand down the chain until the thumb and forefinger are gripping the next link that has to be attached to the hook, be it the second, third or fourth. (The choice of that link may be experimental when the bridle is first fitted.) Then attach that second link to the hook *with your thumbnail down*. Provided the off side attachment is correct, the sequence on the near side is always the same and is always foolproof: *thumbnail up; thumbnail down.*

The next point to remember is that the shape and weight of the curb bit and its rein ensures that there is always a tiny element of lever pressure on the bars of the mouth even when the rider is exerting no significant pressure on the rein. To that extent, and even when riding with a loose curb rein, the bit will of its own accord be 'whispering' the appropriate signals to the horse. But as contact is taken up, so that whisper will become louder and clearer.

The more the bit can be left to operate itself as just described, the less likely will the rider be to fall into the trap of maintaining a dull and permanent pressure on it. That pitfall is easy enough to fall into, not least because the rider usually has many other things to think about, but it is bound to be wholly counter-productive of the gentle response that we hope will become a matter of habit with the horse. If the bit

Fig 41   To fit the curb chain, the hand places the end link on to the left hook with the thumbnail up *in a clockwise movement.*

Fig 42   *The next link (according to the individual fitting chosen) is placed on to the same hook* with the thumbnail down *in an anti-clockwise movement.*

Fig 43 *The curb chain fitted correctly, enabling the metal bit cheek to form an angle of about 25 degrees from the jaw when pulled taut.*

is to operate itself in a steady manner, the chain must be in steady contact with the chin groove. It follows that provided the rider does not misuse the power at his disposal, it is better to have the curb chain fitted in a manner that may appear a little on the tight side, rather than too loose. Then the bit will remain steady in one position. On the other hand, if the rider is not good enough to maintain consistent and sufficient control of his hands to allow the bit that degree of freedom, he should probably not use a double bridle at all.

Loose-Fitting Chains

If the curb chain is fitted too loosely, the bit's function will be progressively destroyed, as the fitting of the chain permits the cheek of the bit to be pulled back to an angle greater than 35–45 degrees from the line of the jaw. The tighter the chain, the less the cheek can be pulled back, and vice versa. Ultimately, as the cheek comes back to 90 degrees, there will be no lever action at all. The bar of the bit, pivoting round the junction of the cheek with the headstall, will then tend to slide

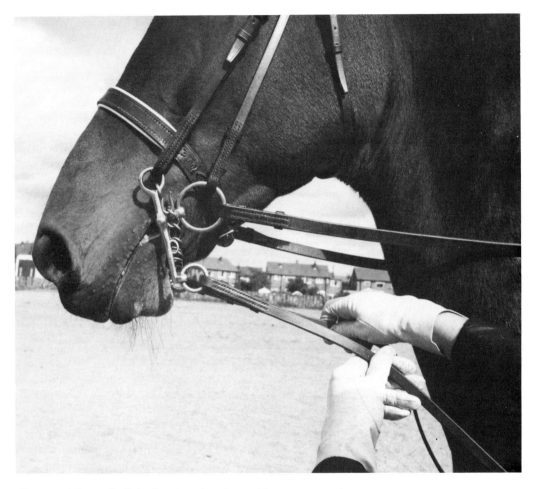

Fig 44 The curb chain fitted too loosely, enabling an approximate 50-degree angle to be formed.

upwards in the mouth so that it interferes with the bridoon. As the line of the cheek becomes identical with that of the rein, the action will degenerate into that of an additional, second-rate and rather cumbersome snaffle. In the intermediate stages, the increased angle of the upper cheekpiece will exert, through the headstall, a degree of downward pressure on the poll that will tend to induce an undesirable lowering of that region. For these reasons, a too-loose curb chain, with the bit cheeks coming back to more than a maximum of 45 degrees to the mouth, will be a clear indication not of kindness to the horse but of the fact that the rider does not know his job or has been careless in fitting his bridle.

There is another and more dangerous effect of a too-loose curb chain. Some bits are made, or can be obtained by unscrupulous riders, with a comparatively high

Fig 45 Here the curb chain is fitted so loosely that the metal cheek is more or less in the same line as the rein, the curb chain therefore having no effect at all.

port, perhaps 1½ in or more in height. The object of a port, at least in theory, is to allow extra room for the tongue to be moved under the bars of the bit. When the bit lies in its normal position without rein tension, the port will lie virtually flat along the tongue, pointing up towards the throat. But the more the lower cheek is pulled back, the more the port is raised off the tongue by the revolving bar, and the closer the top of it will come towards the soft palate which is often flat and flush with the upper gums. It is clear that a loose curb chain can quite easily result in the top of a high port scraping the palate and very quickly making it extremely sore and painful. This unfortunate action has, indeed, been used deliberately over the centuries, and even quite recently, by inhumane riders in order to make their horses 'light in the hand'. In fact, the horses become terrified of any contact by the curb rein and try to keep their mouths as wide open as the noseband permits. The moral must be that the humane rider must make sure he uses a bit with the minimum of port height.

Reciprocal Responses

The key to the happy and correct use of a double bridle lies in the rider's ability and skill in never holding on to the pressure of the curb. He must expect, and indeed demand, a response from the horse to the initial light pressure and must then immediately reciprocate, thus effectively saying 'thank you'. The horse will take the point and be happy to relax his jaw on request and, when relaxed, will invariably become light in hand. And that is the sole legitimate object of a double bridle. It is that soft relaxation, always accompanied by a movement of the tongue (the French *mise en main*) that the rider, with still seat and steady hands, asks for, receives and gives back to his horse. It is done by the use of the fingers alone.

There are certain factors that may make it easier for the rider to achieve this ideal situation in which he and his horse appear to co-operate in the pleasures of lightness. First it is necessary to hold the reins in a manner that best facilitates their sensitive and separate use. The most commonly used manner is that shown in Fig 46. This, however, incorporates one major disadvantage in that both the bridoon and the curb rein are gripped firmly together between the thumb and first finger, thus severely limiting the amount of independent play that can be used with the curb, and also making it difficult to make adjustments to the length of only one rein.

The disadvantages inherent in the common method can be almost totally overcome if the reins are held as in Fig 47. In this case, the bridoon and the curb reins remain separated at all times, and it is only possible to exert the lightest of grips on the curb rein, the loose end of which now passes by itself between the first and second fingers. In practice, there is no need to exert any grip at all at this point, leaving the rein to hang by its own weight within and around the two central fingers, so that the rider may exert extra pressure on the bit by closing his fingers, if necessary.

The length of the curb rein can easily be adjusted by the other hand without in any way affecting the bridoon rein. Also, a much greater amount of give and take with the curb rein can be achieved by the two middle fingers that hold it than is possible by the third finger working alone (Fig 47) and with the loose end of the rein firmly gripped by the thumb. In fact, the rider will find that he can exert as firm a contact as he likes with the bridoon and yet play the curb rein with great sensitivity or without, if he so wishes, putting any pressure on it at all.

Summary

To a very large extent, and with a properly trained rider and horse, the curb rein can be left to look after and to operate itself for most of the time, with no more than the weight of the leather rein providing the contact with the hand. The rein may appear almost loose and will certainly be noticeably less taut than that of the bridoon, but the bit will influence the horse by its existence, its weight and its shape. Used in this way:

Fig 46   *The most common way of holding the reins. The bridoon rein is outside the little finger and the curb rein between it and the third finger. Both spare ends of rein are held between thumb and first finger. This method severely limits the amount of independent play that can be used with the curb and makes it difficult to adjust the length of only one rein.*

Fig 47   *Here the bridoon rein is outside the little finger and is held between the thumb and first finger. The curb rein is held independently by the two middle fingers, passing between the little and third fingers and the second and first fingers. The advantages of this method are explained in the text.*

1. There is no danger of exerting more pressure than is intended.

2. The horse will be conscious of no undue restriction to its head and neck.

3. The weight and shape of the bit itself will gently and constantly whisper reminders to the horse to keep its jaw relaxed.

4. Should the horse suddenly raise its head and come 'above the bit', it will itself cause the bit to operate more strongly by the change in the angle between the rein and the jaw. Horses always know when any kind of discomfort has been caused by their own as opposed to a human action, and will invariably and quite calmly take appropriate steps to avoid a recurrence. In this case, the horse will show none of the resentment that would arise if the rider had suddenly and unexpectedly jerked the curb bit against the mouth.

With a double bridle, the main controlling contact with the mouth should always be through the bridoon, the curb bit being regarded more as a reserve and as a gentle and occasional reminder that is activated by closing more firmly those two central fingers (Fig 47).

8 The Pelham Bit

by Stella Harries

The Pelham bit, which takes its name from the Pelham family, is essentially a bit of the nineteenth and twentieth centuries. There is evidence of earlier curb bits conforming to the single mouthpiece concept and fitted with an additional snaffle ring in the Neapolitan school of the Renaissance, but it was the years between the second half of the nineteenth century and the Second World War which witnessed the growth of the Pelham bit in a quite astonishing variety of ways. Indeed, the Pelham permutations were almost as numerous as those of the basic snaffle bit.

The direct derivation of the Pelham is from the curb bit which was known and used by Rome's Celtic auxiliaries in the second century AD. The bridoon, at first known as the 'flying trench', came to be used in conjunction with the curb during the early Renaissance period and it is possible that it was known in the Byzantine circuses which preceded the establishment of the Neapolitan schools.

The Pelham, by virtue of the upper bridoon or snaffle ring attached to the cheek above and below the mouthpiece, eliminates the use of the separate bridoon lying in the mouth above the curb mouthpiece and incorporated into the bridle by its own sliphead. The bit seeks, by this arrangement, to produce the action of the double bridle (that is, curb and bridoon) whilst employing a single mouthpiece. In

theory this is not possible, nor is it in practice either. Nonetheless, the imprecise and far less direct action of the Pelham appears to be acceptable to many horses. In fact, for horses with short, wide jaws, a conformation often found in the cobby sorts, a Pelham may be an ideal solution. Such horses can rarely accommodate a double bridle comfortably because of their jaw formation. Conversely, it may not be possible to use a Pelham on some Thoroughbred horses for the opposite reason. Because the jaws are long it will be difficult to fit the Pelham correctly (with the lips just wrinkled) without the curb chain riding up out of the curb groove and bearing upon the virtually unprotected jawbones.

The action of the curb bit varies in accordance with its construction. Long cheeks provide the possibility of greater leverage, mouthpieces apply varying degrees of pressure on bars and tongue according to their shape, and so on. The greater the length of the cheek below the mouthpiece, the greater is the possible leverage which can be exerted on the lower jaw. The greater the length of the cheek above the mouthpiece, the greater will be the degree of pressure which can be exerted on the poll.

Shallow ports allow the mouthpiece to act across the lower jaw with the pressure being applied more on the tongue than on the bars. Conversely, a high port, into

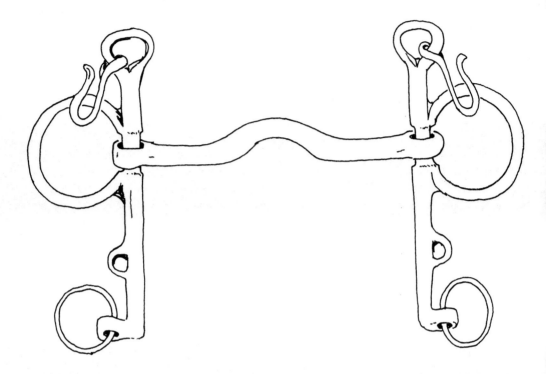

Fig 48   A Pelham with a mouthpiece having a moderately high port.

which the tongue rises, allows the bearing surface of the mouthpiece to bear more directly on the bars. The choice of a mouthpiece should, in consequence, be governed by the conformation of the bar. To remove all pressure from the bars a reverse arch mouthpiece can be used.

In the simplest terms the curb bit, by acting across the lower jaw, at the curb groove and on the poll, causes the head to be lowered, the lower jaw to be relaxed and the nose retracted. The bridoon, again in the very simplest of terms, acts upwards against the corners of the lips to raise the head. By balancing these opposing effects the rider can 'suggest' a head carriage with far greater finesse than with other bitting arrangements – something which is not so easily accomplished, if

indeed it is at all, with the single mouthpiece Pelham.

The position of the reins in the hand does, of course, have an effect upon the action. If the snaffle rein is held outside the little finger it could be said that its action predominates. The reins held in the opposite fashion emphasise the actions of the curb bit. Held in the French fashion, with the bridoon between the third and fourth finger and the curb rein under the little finger, the emphasis is again more to the curb, but positioning the reins in the hand corresponding to the position of the bridoon and curb in the mouth is really more logical.

All these observations can be applied to the Pelham, but because one mouthpiece attempts to fulfil the functions of the

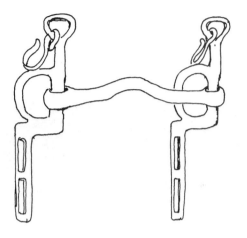

Fig 49   The Reversible, Angle-cheek or Universal Pelham.

curb/bridoon combination, it is a far less precise instrument. On the other hand, the inexperienced can do less damage with a Pelham than with a double bridle. For that reason the army devised the army reversible, or Angle-cheek Pelham. This was a bit which provided sufficient alternatives to cope with most troop horses. For light-mouthed horses the curb rein could be fitted to the centre slot, whilst for horses taking a stronger hold the curb rein went to the bottom one. Additionally, the mouthpiece was smooth on one side and rough on the other.

Any mouthpiece which is used in a

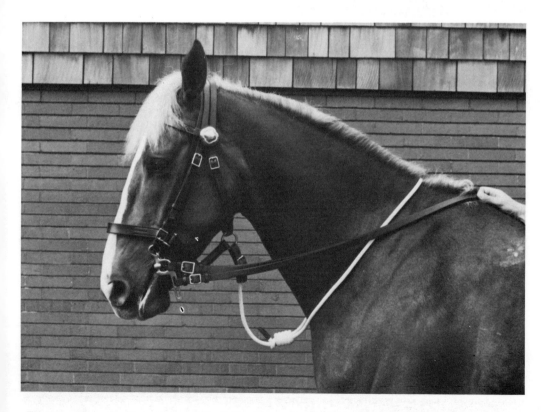

Fig 50   Here the Army Reversible Pelham is used on a police horse's bridle with the curb rein fitted to the centre slot.

Fig 51   This photograph demonstrates the versatility of the police bridle, which can be quickly converted into a headcollar without having to unbridle the horse and put on a separate headcollar.

Fig 52   The Scamperdale Pelham.

curb bit can be employed in a Pelham, with one or two exceptions. A Banbury mouthpiece, for instance, would present difficulties. On the other hand there are mouthpieces which belong entirely to the Pelham family and could not be incorporated into a curb/bridoon combination – the Scamperdale, developed by the late Sam Marsh, is an example, as is the Rugby Pelham, a favourite polo bit.

One of the disadvantages of the Pelham is that the eyes of the bit are prone to chafe unless bent outwards away from the horse's cheek. The Scamperdale overcame this fault by 'elbowing' the ends of the straight bar mouthpiece so that the eyes were placed that much further to the rear. The Rugby Pelham, with a loose bridoon ring connected to the bit by a link, is perhaps closer than anything else to the occasional examples of the Pelham-type bit found in the early classical schools. Rarely, however, is it used as it was intended. For it to give a greater upward force to the bit, the bridoon ring should be suspended from a sliphead.

A plain, centrally-jointed mouthpiece is found only in the Pelham (the snaffle being excepted) and it has to be accounted as one of the least logical mouth constructions in a family of bits in which illogicalities abound. The single-rein ported Kimblewick is also a member of the Pelham group. Originally, this was termed the Spanish jumping bit, but it acquired its new name when it was taken up by Phil Oliver, father of Allan, who lived at Kimblewick.

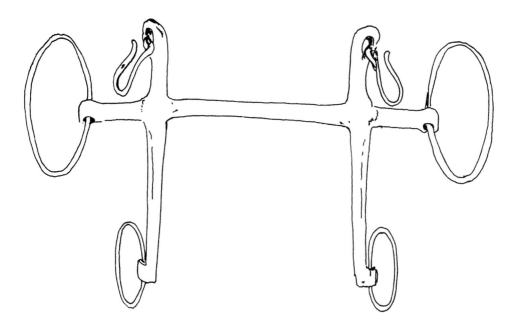

Fig 53   The Rugby Pelham.

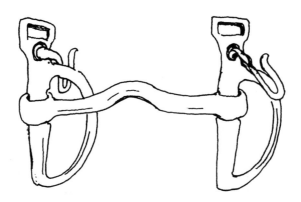

Fig 54   A Kimblewick with the usual ported mouthpiece
(known as the Kimberwick in the USA).

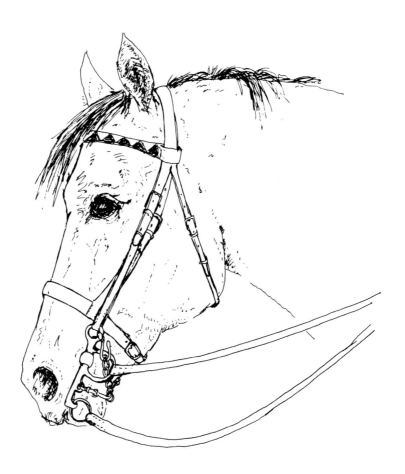

Fig 55   It is usual, though not mandatory, for the curb chain to be passed through the bridoon rings, encouraging a more direct action and helping prevent the chain rising out of the curb/chin groove.

The action of the bit depends largely upon the position of the hands. If they are dropped prior to pressure being applied to the rein, the rein will slide about 1 in down the D-shaped cheek. The bit then assumes a position of 45 degrees in the mouth which causes the mouthpiece to bear downwards across the lower jaw and to the rear. The action is assisted by the square eye, to which the cheekpiece of the bridle is attached, and exerts a transmitted lowering pressure to the poll.

In almost every instance it is advisable for the curb chain of a Pelham to be passed through the bridoon rings. This encourages a more direct action and combats, to a degree, the tendency for the chain to rise out of the curb groove, even though a lipstrap may be fitted.

9 Riding on the Curb

by Sylvia Stanier, LVO

History

It appears from the historical records available that bits can be divided into two geographical areas. Looking at paintings, sculptures and carvings dating right back before Christ and thence through the centuries to the fourteenth and fifteenth centuries AD, a distinct pattern emerges. The peoples to the north and east of Europe and Central Asia – even the Chinese – rode in the equivalent of a snaffle whilst those people emanating from Arabia, North Africa, and later Spain and Italy, used a curb. Cossacks, for instance, and Genghis Khan's hordes all used a snaffle; the Arabians, Syrians and Moors used a form of curb.

As the Moors moved into Spain, so the curb bit arrived in Europe. At the same time the 'snaffle' people of eastern Europe and the steppes were rather less successful in their ascendancy to power. After the defeat of the Moors by Ferdinand and Isabella of Castille in 1492, it was inevitable that, after 400 years of Moorish domination, much Moorish influence should remain. Thus, it appears that the Andalusian type of horse was equipped with a basically Moorish bit, that is the curb.

The Andalusian horse became the most important riding horse in Europe. Spain was probably the most important country in Europe and also, as the dis-

Fig 56 A very old ring bit with an enormously large port. The ring acted as a curb chain would, by surrounding the lower jaw.

85

Fig 57 The ring bit from the side, with the ring in the position it would be in use. The horse's lower jaw would pass down through the ring under the mouth-piece.

coverer of the New World, the most important influence on society at large during the fifteenth and sixteenth centuries.

The Renaissance of the sixteenth century brought power to France and Italy. In an age of nobility, wealth and innovation, horse riding became more than a mode of transport. The carrousel became a popular entertainment. Young gentlemen studied with Monsieur de Pluvinel not only the art of equitation but the arts in general. A more sophisticated form of

equitation developed, using the fashionable Spanish horse with its Moorish bit. These bits became more and more fanciful, at least with the decorations on the arm or lever. Often, however, the mouthpieces remained relatively soft (that is, the cannons were thick and uncomplicated whilst the reins, the headpiece and other pieces of saddlery were extremely ornate).

Two other points emerge along the way. One is that the Spanish had introduced horses to the New World, and thus emanated the Canadian cutting horse, the North American roping horse, the Mexican charro horse, the Peruvian paso horse and the Argentinian polo ponies (criollos), all of which are ridden in some form of curb bit.

Secondly, the wars in Europe saw the increasing use of cavalry. The footsoldier, or infantry man, sought the best way to unseat his mounted adversary, and found that nothing was easier than to cut the horse's reins. So, to counteract this, chains and longer cheeks were attached to the outside of the mouthpiece. With the Spanish type of horse, the distance from the horse's mouth to its neck was short, so rein-cutting would be minimised by a long cheek and some chain attached to the ordinary leather rein held in the hand.

This useful combination leads us to François Robichon de la Guérinière – the father of dressage, the inventor of the shoulder-in, the writer of *Ecole de Cavalerie*, and the greatest equestrian master of the early eighteenth century. He also used a special curb bit based on the soft mouthpiece, long cheek and part chain rein. Being an artist and an innovator, he decided to balance his bits as well as his horses. As well as the bit, he used a form of bosal or noseband to help with this balancing.

The turning point between the snaffle and the curb was something we have heard so much about in our own century – speed. Beside the evolution of the English racehorse stood the need for faster warfare as the age of Napoleon began, and the fashions of fox-hunting and parading in the Bois de Boulogne not on a Spanish horse but on an English Thoroughbred became more popular. The gentry of England and, to a large extent, Germany, did expect their fully-trained 'hacks' to go to perfection in a double bridle, but the snaffle was creeping in. Then showjumping became fashionable and Caprilli, after much fuss with the authorities, became the supreme master of the snaffle and the jump. So what of the curb? It went out of fashion, and fashion is a very hard thing to break!

Now, however, we are told to train our horses in a snaffle, but it is imperative that the well-trained dressage horse, parade horse or Western horse must still obey the curb rules. The curb is still the ultimate aim – although it is very often feared and misunderstood.

How it Works

A curb bit works from leverage, that is, as the cheekpiece moves backwards the curb chain comes into play. The longer the cheekpiece (or shank, as it is known in the USA) the more severe the action. There is also pressure on top of the horse's head – the poll – so the two need to be co-ordinated and balanced. The longer the cheekpiece, the stronger the downward leverage; the longer the upper cheekpiece the more poll pressure. The

curb chain itself should be of a certain width and tension. It all sounds very difficult, but in fact the principle is quite simple.

Does your horse pull, lean, or get its tongue over the bit? Do you like a strong contact or a light one? All these things can be worked out according to your horse's conformation and your requirements. I prefer a light contact but, having said that, I can only have as light a contact as my horse will accept. Compromise and schooling are relevant. If the horse gets his tongue over the bit then a larger port may be advisable.

The reining horses of the USA are trained to go on a bosal and then, when fully trained, they are put into a curb bit. The rider will have trained the horse through leg and body aids – he will use no hand aids at all. The charro rider does much the same and uses the chains of the curb bit to balance his hand to 'give' rather than 'take' the rein – using no backward tension. The Spanish and Portuguese riders use a very fine featherlight heel and leg aid – not so much a body and back aid – in the tradition of Marialva, the great Portuguese trainer of the eighteenth century.

So, the purpose of the curb bit is simply for balance. It comes into effect according to the length of the cheek, the tightness of the curb chain and the ability of the rider to sit still, yet ask the horse to obey his heel (and spur) command. There must be no backward tension or pulling on the reins.

The weight and angle of the bit will affect the work – I have a bit I brought from California some years ago which is weighted and balanced for an 'average' horse. The man who made it was horrified that I couldn't bring the horse to have

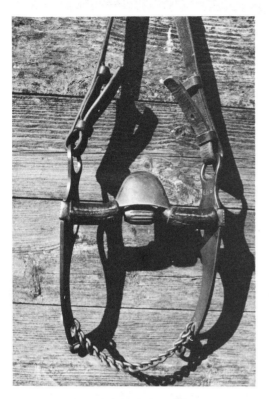

*Fig 58 A Spanish spade bit with a
high copper port and copper central
roller (cricket). This particular bit has
the cannons covered with leather. It
would normally have either a metal curb
chain or leather curb strap to ensure
leverage.*

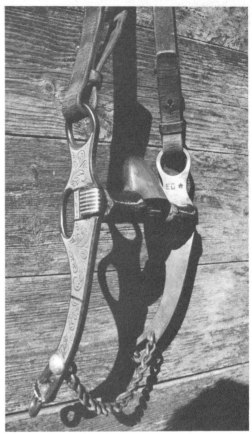

*Fig 59 The same bit from the side.
Note the engravings on the arm or shank
(cheekpiece).*

its mouth measured! He was right – each
horse *should* have a special bit only for
him.

The criteria for success in riding with a
curb bit only are:

1.   Not to pull on the bit.
2.   To see that the bit rests comfortably
in the horse's mouth.
3.   To see that the bit is neither too
narrow nor too wide. If too wide, the
curb chain will come into play on the jaw

bones only instead of encircling the outside of the lower jaw evenly.

You must also have a supple wrist. Most
times, the reins of a curb bit bridle are
held in the left hand; turning the wrist
therefore turns the reins and co-ordinates
the leg and hand aids. The speed of a polo
pony or a Western horse can be considerable; stopping from full gallop or turning
at full gallop needs skill and excellent
balance, as things happen very quickly.

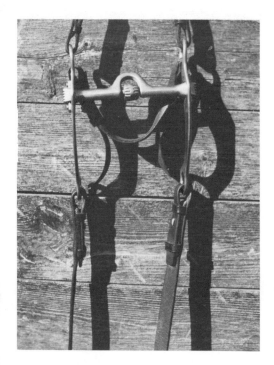

Fig 60 *A Western bit with a medium port and a copper roller (cricket). A leather curb strap is attached.*

Fig 61 *The Western bit from the side.*

In a parade horse, work is done at a slow walk, which, in some cases, is annoying for a horse, so tact is again needed to see that movements are carried out smoothly.

Aids and Uses

I like to teach all my horses to stop to a closing of my knees into the saddle, thus minimising the use of the reins, and only keeping as light and even a tension on them as possible. To tell the horse to stop, straighten your back and close your knees.

To turn, look the way you want to go and, if turning left, for instance, look left,

place your right leg further behind the girth than your left one and carry your hand (and reins) to the left – thus applying a slight 'neck-rein' effect. Depending on your chosen subject – polo, Western riding, parade work, or even High School dressage – it is essential that your horse performs certain movements. In polo, for example, when the horse must stop, turn and gallop, all at great speed, it is often necessary to attach other reins and nosebands to help achieve success.

The Doma Vacquero horses (cowponies of Spain) are ridden with a curb bit and a low noseband, which helps again to stop and turn these horses at speed without hurting their mouths. In the parade horse, due to army regulations, such

89

*Fig 62   The author of this chapter riding Leopardo on the curb
rein of a simple double bridle, with the reins in the left hand
and the whip in the right hand in the traditional (upright)
position, whereby it can be used on either side of the horse
without having to be changed from hand to hand. The horse is
moving in an uncollected, although well balanced, pace, hence his
whole outline is longer than if he was collected.*

'helps' as extra nosebands are not allowed
– the horse must go in the bridle which is
the uniform of his regiment. This can
lead to difficulties; the horses have to be
well schooled by the various Riding
Masters so as to become used to this
discipline before being ridden by any
important person. The Western horse has
a slightly easier task in that it is usually
ridden by a skilled rider who understands
balance and lightness of hand, plus the use

of sensible leg and body (weight) aids.

Each of the horses mentioned above
must not only be able to stop and turn but
also perform a 'full pass' either way,
certainly at walk (for the parade and
police horses) and often at trot and canter
for the Western and the Doma Vacquero
– it is almost a basic movement for them.
On parade, you cannot come and make a
full circle to reposition yourself sideways; the horse must learn to side-step.

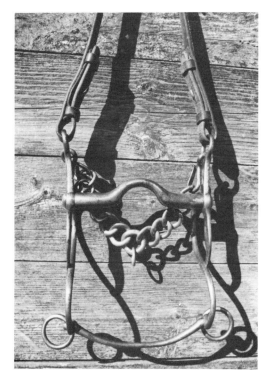

Fig 63   A cavalry officer's bit. This bit can be used with either one or two reins or as part of a double bridle. It would normally have a regimental badge attached to the side-pieces.

Fig 64   The same military bit from the side.

Similarly, the horse working cattle must side-step to prevent the calf from escaping.

I recommend that you introduce your horse carefully to these movements at the walk, and later go on into the faster paces if required. Patience and understanding are essential, as in all forms of riding. Self-balance in the horse is very important

indeed if you wish to ride off the curb only. A saddle in which you can sit fairly deeply may be helpful but try and sit lightly and softly so as to find your point of balance on the horse. This will help the horse to find its own balance with you on board a little more easily and lessen the feeling of wanting to pull on the reins.

10 Schooling Accessories, Martingales and Nosebands

by Molly Sivewright, FIH, FBHS, FABRS

It is not easy for me to write a chapter about what are usually called 'gadgets' because, generally, my hackles rise at the mention of the word! However, as I am often advising those I teach, be they riders, budding instructors or eminent judges, to 'look for the good first', I realise that I must apply my own maxim to myself. To find out what is good about gadgets and how to tell whether they are useful or harmful we must look to the horse as well as the trainer who uses the gadget. We must decide if the horse needs it, and if the trainer is capable of using it.

The horse is a large and powerful animal; he has an excellent memory which, unfortunately, stores up those events which he should not store up just as well as those which he should retain. The trainer may be large and powerful but he is very unlikely to be a match for the size and strength of the horse, even if he is a potential Mr Atlas! If the horse succeeds in defying his trainer's wishes, he will always remember that success just as well as he will remember the pleasure he feels when he has pleased his trainer. If the defiance is allowed to continue or if resistance is met by brute force, the situation will deteriorate and the trainer

will soon have a 'rogue' on his hands.

Unfortunately, the tempo of our modern life is unnaturally rushed, time is at a premium, and good horses are expensive to buy and to keep, so the pressure is on, often to the detriment of the horse's well-being as well as his training. Because young, untrained or partially trained horses command a lower purchase price than those who have been well schooled, the former are often bought by inexperienced purchasers, sometimes for their equally inexperienced offspring. All of this results in a 'blind leading the blind' situation.

When horses have had a bad experience of any sort, they will require many weeks or months of careful handling and reschooling by a knowledgeable and experienced trainer to restore their confidence, obedience and form. The use of gadgets should be reserved for these experts exclusively; when used by inexperienced riders, most gadgets can truthfully be likened to a razor blade in the hands of a monkey.

The general purpose of any gadget is to increase the trainer's chances of success in the event of a disagreement between himself and his horse. Most gadgets are designed to increase the clarity and the strength of the rider's aids or signals. If used occasionally, only when the need arises, and then with great tact, a few, intelligently designed gadgets can have a use – one at a time.

Bad gadgets are those which are rigid and forceful, by means of which so-called trainers tie up their horses into a set shape which they consider to be a correct form, whereas in reality they are contorting their horses' minds and muscles and ruining their true, natural action. These pseudo-trainers fail to appreciate that the true qualities of mental and physical balance and unconstraint combined with free, forward movement, suppleness, obedience and impulsion are essential factors in the development of the riding horse. Only if these qualities are preserved can there be a correct development of the horse's trunk muscles and an improvement in his posture, enabling him to carry his rider with ease and to move his limbs with maximum efficiency and beauty of movement. Good form can only exist if the horse is happy, confident and muscularly fit and athletic; it can never be found in horses which have been forced, restricted and made anxious or cowed.

There are many books in circulation today which describe in detail a variety of gadgets, some invented by our forefathers and quite a number of more modern contraptions too. It serves no real purpose to try to compile the longest-ever list of gadgets; rather it will be more useful to select a few which have a certain popularity at present, a few of which may have a use in rare and exceptional cases, and offer some basic dos and don'ts.

Training Aids

Basic Tackle

It must be understood that a normal young horse will never require any equipment beyond the basic tackle and saddlery respectively for his lungeing, backing and riding away. Only if the preliminary or subsequent stages of training are carried out with too little thought or a lack of expertise will a good trainer even contemplate using a gadget to help him to reschool a spoiled horse.

'Breaking tackle' is a most unpleasant label, conjuring up, as it does, visions of horses' spirits being broken by rough methods, dumb-jockeys, bearing reins, tortured minds and muscles and a cowed horse forced into quaking submission. We should train our young horses, not 'break' them. Thus, we should follow the preliminary handling, leading and general mannering and acclimatisation procedures with a programme of work on the lunge-line.

The basic tackle for the early stages of training the young horse is:

1. A light, well-padded lunge-cavesson.
2. A mild jointed snaffle bit in a bridle without a noseband.
3. A lunge-line.
4. A lunge-whip.
5. A training roller fitted with a breast-girth.
6. Protective boots.

Most of the other optional appendages could be classified as gadgets, with the two following exceptions.

Fig 66 Lungeing equipment. The cavesson's nose-band is fully padded and, therefore, goes above the bit and inside the bridle cheek-straps to leave the bit free and comfortable. (The horse wears a D-ring snaffle.) The jowl-strap is fitted tightly enough to prevent the cheek straps from being pulled forward too near to the horse's eye. The side-reins are solid, lightweight and fully adjustable. The leather roller is stout and strong but very supple; it has an extra thick felt pad under the top pads and a crupper to hold it back into place behind the horse's shoulder blades. The crupper is well padded with sheepskin and has two small buckles at the front of the tail-piece as well as the main length-adjusting buckle in front of the croup. (The small Welsh friend is clearly saying: 'Don't forget the breast-girth, boots and lunge whip!')

The Crupper

A crupper is an essential addition to the lungeing equipment. The purpose is to keep the roller back behind the horse's shoulder-blades, thereby encouraging free development of the horse's shoulder-girdle muscles in front of the roller. The value of this will stand the horse and its rider in good stead for the whole of the horse's life:

1. The saddle will stay back in its correct place even when cantering or bounding down the steepest hill.
2. The horse's shoulders and forelimbs are allowed the maximum freedom of movement.
3. The shoulder blades, being uncramped by a saddle which has moved forward on to them, are not restricted by it and they can 'open', thus allowing the front of the trunk to be lifted up and enabling the hind limbs to be engaged further forward under the horse's body mass.
4. The front portions of the horse's *latissimus dorsi* muscles are unhindered in their action of connecting the horse's fore and hind limbs through his trunk.
5. The rider will never need to buy a fore-girth!

A training crupper should have two buckles on either side of the tailpiece as well as on the back strap itself. The tailpiece should be comfortably padded with sheepskin and the young horse should have been accustomed to wearing a tail bandage before a crupper is fitted. It should be fitted comfortably rather than tightly for the first few days, after which it may be adjusted to keep the roller back in the required position. An inexperienced eye will invariably have difficulty in judging how far back the roller and later the saddle should sit.

Side-Reins

Side-reins may be fitted for any of the following reasons:

1. To encourage the horse to work straight – even on curved lines, he should follow his nose exactly and work both sides of his body equally.
2. To help to contain his thoughts to work with his trainer rather than his attention being diverted by outside distractions.
3. To accustom the horse to the bit and the weight of the reins on the bit.
4. In later stages of his training, side-reins are useful when the trainer works the horse in hand.
5. When retraining spoiled horses, side-reins will assist the trainer to control a large, obstreperous horse or one who has been badly started and has learned how to baffle his trainer by turning quickly inwards or outwards whenever he does not wish to continue working on the lunge.
6. An inexperienced lunger will find it easier to work a horse between his forward-driving and restraining aids if the horse wears side-reins.
7. They may also be useful when giving a pupil a lunge lesson.
8. On the Continent, beginner riders' horses have side-reins fitted when riding without reins in early lessons, until the instructor deems that the riders' seats are sufficiently balanced and steady to permit them to ride with their bridle reins.

Side-reins are fitted from the side rings on the cavesson or from the snaffle rings to the roller. They should never be fitted so tight that they impede the horse's natural gaits; nor should they be fitted so loose and low that there is any danger of a horse putting a forefoot over a side-rein. Low side-reins can be too severe in their action and may encourage the horse to go too deep and on his forehand. Side-reins which are crossed over in front of the withers restrict the use of the *ligamentum nuchae* and the related muscles and often cause a shortening rather than a lengthening of the horse's top line, especially in his neck, and his back will be slack.

Side-reins may be wholly elasticated, made of leather with a rubber or elastic insert, or they may be solid, that is made entirely of leather or webbing with no elastic inserts. If I am going to use side-reins, I prefer the solid type as those with elastic often encourage horses to test the contact of the rider's rein aids by means of little (or large) pulls. Side-reins should be strong but light, easy to unfasten quickly and they should never be fitted too tight. They should be removed for work at walk and over fences, and whenever a rider is mounting.

Gadgets

The crupper and side-reins are more truly described as training aids; the use of the following gadgets must be more carefully considered, if they are used at all.

The Chambon

A chambon is of French origin, having the name of its inventor. Fig 66 shows how the horse moves freely while the chambon dissuades a spoiled horse from adopting a tense, head-high, hollow-backed posture with a stiff-legged, 'running' action.

The chambon can have a use in the

Fig 66   A chambon fitted for lungeing. The horse shows that its influence is felt even when the chambon looks quite slack. It should not be fitted tighter 'to fix the horse into a low outline'.

restraining of a spoiled horse, helping him to regain confidence, to work 'long and low' with a rounded top line and a restored spring in the trot. It encourages the horse to relax, be supple and to work in a correct form.

A chambon should be used with great discretion and tact; at first it should be fitted loosely while the horse gets used to its action, little by little, as he is lunged. It should never be put on in the stable, it should always be comfortable – never forcibly tight – and it should never be fitted when the horse is ridden. The chambon is designed and intended for lungeing only, as a temporary measure for short periods.

Running Reins

Running or sliding reins may be used for lungeing as a more free form of side-reins. Trainers who favour running reins hope that their use will persuade the horse to seek the bit and work 'long and low'. When an expert is working the horse, running reins can produce the desired effect.

Overhead Checks

Overhead checks, or bearing reins, should never be used. The only exception to this rule is that a near-relation, known as grass reins, can be useful when children are learning the techniques of lungeing on ponies who far prefer grazing to working on the lunge! Absolutely no benefit can be gained from fitting gadgets which aim at forcing the horse to carry his head in an artificially raised attitude. As was mentioned earlier, we must encourage the horse to lift the front of his trunk, and he can only develop the

muscular means to do this if he is allowed to stretch his top line and to employ his head and neck to assist the use of his back and trunk muscles and to engage his hind legs further forward.

New Gadgets for Old

The practice of fitting tight head-raising gadgets will invariably result in permanent damage to the horse's frame, his form and his gaits. Fortunately, other training gadgets such as dumb-jockeys, the Disdas tackle and the Barnum restraining tackle are all obsolete museum pieces and that is the best place for them! Originally, they were designed for the old-fashioned 'nagsmen' who had more young horses to train than they themselves could ride, thus they did a great deal of preliminary mannering and educating from the ground and many good, sound young hunters they produced. Unfortunately, as is so often the case, these carefully designed contraptions became instruments of torture when used by pseudo-trainers who lacked the knowledge and horse-sense to use them with kindness and discretion.

In these modern times, the training scene is much the same; modern monstrosities have replaced some of the obsolete gadgets. The 'get rich quick' boys dazzle the inexperienced horseowner with flashy advertisements and tales of remarkably speedy horse production, with top lines made in a month or less. As before, the horse suffers – he cannot explain the mental and physical agonies he is forced to endure.

Tragically, the end result of such work will be a disaster for both the owner, who has wasted so much time, money and energy, and for the horse who has suffered to no avail. The much pro-claimed top line will not exist. In its place will be tense ridges of muscle on either side of the horse's neck and back which can take a year to disperse. How much wiser and more beneficial it would have been for both partners if the owner had expended the time, money and energy on some good training for himself so that he would have had no need to use a gim-micky gadget on his horse.

There is another group of gadgets to consider, those used as training aids for the ridden horse. The novice horseowner may well ask, 'How do I know a good gadget from a bad gadget?' At least he knows that there *are* bad gadgets; he must understand that he should seek advice before purchasing any extra piece of saddlery. If there is no expert living locally, he can write for an official dress-age rule book which will provide him with a list of permitted saddlery. (He need not be over-awed by the word dressage – it is a useful little label for looking after, training and riding the horse!)

Martingales

There are at least ten different sorts of martingale, the most useful of which is probably the running martingale.

Running Martingales

The make and shape of the running martingale is shown in Fig 67, and, as with all martingales, it must be fitted correctly. Normally, the rings should be able to reach the top of the horse's withers; if the rider rides side-saddle, the ring should reach a hand's breadth above the withers, and in the hands of an expert the martingale may be a hand's breadth shorter than the normal length. If used with a snaffle the bridle should have two reins, one from bit to hand and one passing through the rings of the martin-gale between bit and hand. The rider can then use the rein without the interference of the martingale for the greater part of his work. The martingale ring can cause that rein to snap, even a very well cared-for rein, so the rider needs a 'second string to his bow'!

All martingales should always be fitted with a tight, thick rubber ring, diagonally across the join where the martingale strap runs through the loop at the bottom of the neckstrap, to prevent the main strap from slipping down to form a dangerous loop between the horse's front legs.

The uses of the running martingale are:

1. It helps keep the horse straight by keeping the reins straight from the bit to the rider's hands, even when the horse tosses his head about.
2. It dissuades a horse from tossing his head about.
3. It ensures that the reins stay in place, especially in exciting or stressful circum-stances.
4. It can be useful on some green horses to keep them straight and attentive when riding out of doors, in company, over fences and/or across country.
5. It 'anchors' the neckstrap and pre-vents it from swivelling round the horse's neck if the rider should need the neck-strap's support while riding a green or difficult horse.
6. If a new pupil has a faulty seat and unsteady hands, a running martingale will nullify the uncomfortable jostlings

Fig 67   A running martingale and rubber 'stops' fitted on the billetted reins. The horse is also wearing a flash noseband attached by a small leather loop to the front of the cavesson noseband and fitting snugly but not too tight round the horse's muzzle below the bit.

somewhat before they reach the horse's mouth.

The main disadvantages of a running martingale are twofold:

1.   The martingale rings cause an unwanted interruption on the reins between the rider's hands and the horse's mouth.
2.   A well-trained horse should not need a martingale; some riders can become too

reliant on it and feel quite 'lost' without a martingale.

There are many competitions at which the use of a martingale is barred.

Standing Martingales

The standing martingale is similar to the running martingale except that it is fixed, the back of the cavesson noseband running through the loop at the top of the

Fig 68   A standing martingale fitted loosely on a breastplate.

martingale strap.

The object of the standing martingale is not, as many people think, to pull down the horse's head or to fix it at a lower height than his normal, natural head carriage; rather, the object is to prevent the horse from throwing up his head in a dangerously violent manner and thereby injuring the rider's face or knocking him unconscious. Some trainers believe that a standing martingale should be fitted on to young horses when they are first ridden out as they are then less likely to learn the vice of rearing if they are frightened by some strange object.

The standing martingale should be fitted to reach the top of the gullet-groove. It should never be fitted any

tighter or the horse's head and neck will be too restricted, so that when the martingale is removed the horse will carry his head higher than ever, as if seeking the pressure on his nose. Ideally, the horse should be unaware that he is wearing a standing martingale – unless he tries to throw his head up.

Other Martingales

A Market Harborough may be classified as a martingale or as a rein; in fact, it is both. Providing it is fitted correctly, as shown in Fig 69 (not too tight), the gadget part only comes into play when the horse stiffens his poll and jaw to resist his rider's restraining aids. It is a useful

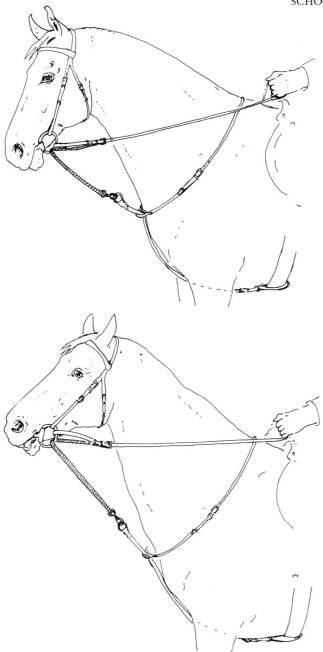

Fig 69(a) The Market Harborough remains in a passive mode when the horse carries his head in the desired position. (b) The Market Harborough comes into action when the horse raises his head too high, encouraging him to bring it down into a more comfortable position.

restraining gadget for the highly-strung, headstrong horse whose training has been rushed.

The Gogue is a martingale-rein designed by Monsieur Gogue, a brother-officer of Monsieur Chambon, both of Saumur, the famous French Cavalry School. It would seem that both designers were guided by the same principle, that is to encourage a spoiled horse to adopt a better form by applying a soft pressure to his poll as well as to his mouth, rather than solely (or rather doubly) on his mouth, as is the case with running reins. Whereas the Chambon is used exclusively for lungeing, the Gogue may be used when the horse is being reschooled under saddle.

There are two varieties of the Gogue, the *independent* (the fixed, martingale type) and the *command* (the more free, rein type). Both should be used with great discretion and in conjunction with the snaffle rein which, of course, will be the main rein influence. If and when the badly-trained horse reverts to an incorrect form of 'Johnny-head-in-air' with a hollow, stiff back, trailing hind legs and awkward leg action to match, the rider may ask the horse to soften in his poll and to employ the top line muscles rather than the muscles in the under part of his neck, by tactful feeling on the Gogue rein. As with all auxiliary gadgets, the Gogue must be used sparingly, kindly and temporarily.

Reins

Running Reins

Running, or sliding, reins are used more often for riding. As may be seen from Fig 71, the running rein is so called because it runs (or slides) through the

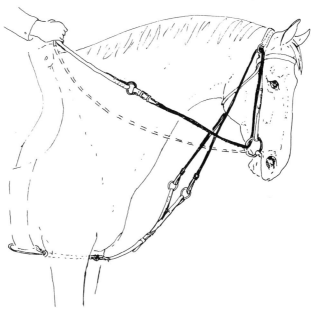

Fig 70 A Gogue of the 'command' type.

Fig 71   Running reins fitted at knee level on either side.

rings of the snaffle bit and thence to the girth, on either side under the saddle flaps or in the girth groove at the back of the sternum. The latter position is more severe and thus can be the most damaging.

Running reins may have an occasional use in the retraining of horses who, as a result of bad training or riding, have learned to go with their heads in the air, backs hollow and hind legs trailing when ridden. An expert may use a running rein as a means of suggesting a more comfortable way of going to his horse. It is most important that the running rein is used only as an occasional suggestion to help the horse to learn to accept the bit with a

supple poll and with a growing confidence and understanding of his rider's signals, particularly of his rein aids.

The ordinary bridle reins should be fully employed in the usual manner, while the running rein is used as seldom as possible to encourage the horse to work in a good form whenever he loses his nerve and becomes tense and resistant. The rider must be extremely tactful when using running reins. He must never use them to fight the horse's resistance and he must reward generously every movement of softening and compliance the horse gives him. Of course, the rider must remember that his forward-driving aids are of the utmost importance in rebuild-

Fig 72   Running reins fitted between the forelegs, the horse demonstrating the danger of over-bending, bringing his nose in behind the vertical even though the running reins are loose!

ing the horse's form and that the horse's head-carriage is the result of his good form – not the beginning of it! And remember that running reins are not draw-reins.

Draw-Reins

Draw-reins are shorter than running reins and they only have one buckle. The centre of the continuous strap lies on or just behind the bridle headpiece from whence it passes through the snaffle bit rings, from outside to inside, and then runs back to the rider's hands. The reins draw the bit up while pressing on the horse's poll, thus their action is similar to that of a gag snaffle. They were used originally to reschool horses who had learned to go on their forehands, lower their heads and lean on the bit. (The wrong sort of 'long and low'!)

Nosebands

The main purposes of a noseband are:

1.   Appearance – a horse looks well-dressed with a noseband and under-dressed without one.

2.   As a training aid to prevent the horse

Fig 73   Draw reins – horse wondering what is coming next!

from resisting or evading the rider's influences by setting his lower jaw and poll against the rider's rein aids, with an open mouth.

Whereas a cavesson noseband is a traditionally 'correct' form of head-wear, as is a skull cap, a bowler hat or a silk hat for the rider, a drop noseband and its near relations are useful and valid training accessories.

Cavesson Nosebands

In most English-speaking countries the cavesson is regarded as the normal nose-band. The recognised fitting is two fingers width below the bottom of the projecting ridge down the side of the horse's cheek-bone, and the breadth of two fingers between the front of the horse's face and the inside of the nose-band. These measurements ensure that there is no risk of the horse's skin being pinched or bruised.

If a cavesson noseband is fitted any tighter than prescribed, then it must be very well padded all round to avoid causing discomfort, or even acute pain and damage to the bones of the horse's face and under its lower jaw. Sometimes a cavesson noseband is over-tightened in

Fig 74   A well-proportioned double bridle with ordinary
cavesson noseband, and bits fitted two holes too high for normal
practice.

order to disguise the fact that the horse's training falls short of the required standard; that he does not accept the bit as thoroughly as he should if the rider's rein aids are to have a soft and smooth effect on the whole of his musculature, posture and movement. Just as a rider's black gloves seem to shout, 'Look, the hands inside us are dead and heavy', so a fluffy piece of sheepskin around the back of a cavesson noseband arouses a warning that all is not well with regard to the horse's acceptance of the bit – that there are mouth and basic training problems.

A cavesson is the sole type of noseband permitted for use with a full or double bridle; it is also the only pattern of noseband to which a standing martingale should be attached.

It is often said that prevention is better than cure, and several nosebands have been designed especially to assist both the trainer and the horse; they are listed below in order of merit.

The Drop Noseband

This noseband is regarded as even more normal than a cavesson noseband in many countries where, if you go to buy a snaffle bridle, you will discover that a drop noseband is included rather than a cavesson noseband.

A drop noseband prevents a horse from opening his mouth too wide, in a rude manner, and thus resisting his rider's influences. If a horse learns to evade the rider's rein aids by going against the bit, opening his mouth and setting his jaw, the bit will slide up into the corners of his mouth, he will roll up his tongue and, as the mouth dries out, it will become less sensitive. This resistance will spread quickly from the jaw to the poll, to the neck, to the back and the joints of the hind legs. It is to avoid such a series of disasters occurring that a drop noseband was designed and is used by many trainers.

It is important that a drop noseband is made correctly, with a reasonably short front strap, supported on both sides by an enclosed, spiked ring to prevent it from drooping down on to the flexible carti-lage at the end of the nasal bone. It should be fitted the breadth of four fingers above the top of the horse's nostrils and with

room for a little more than one finger in the front, between nose and noseband. A drop noseband should never be fitted lower or tighter.

Due to their lower position, these nosebands are more efficient in control-ling the movement of the horse's lower jaw. Conveniently, the chin or curb groove is well shaped to accommodate the back strap of a working noseband, whereas the sharp outer edges of the branches of the lower jaw are not suitable places for pressure of any sort.

The purpose of the drop noseband is not to clamp shut the horse's mouth, nor to impede his breathing. Rather, by pre-venting the horse from opening his mouth too wide, the drop noseband will lessen the likelihood of the bit sliding up out of position and will increase the pro-bability that it will remain resting quietly and correctly on the horse's tongue and the bars of his mouth, from whence the horse is ready to receive, accept and respond to his rider's rein aids.

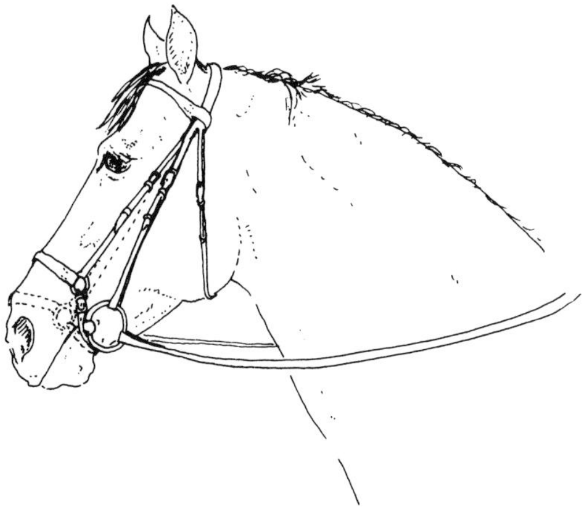

Fig 75 Correctly fitted drop noseband. The dotted line shows the common, incorrect fitting.

The Flash Noseband

The flash noseband is regarded by some trainers as an improvement on a drop noseband, as the front of the noseband is held up most securely by the cavesson noseband to which it is attached by one of two methods. The single, small strap which comprises the flash noseband may be cut in two, the buckle piece being the longer. The two pieces are then sewn on to the centre-front of a stout cavesson noseband, at an angle so that they cross over before being fastened around the lower jaw as in a drop noseband.

Alternatively, a small leather loop may be sewn on to the centre-front of the cavesson noseband through which the flash noseband strap is passed before being fastened as above. The buckle must always be pulled through to the near side. It must never lie in the chin groove where it might damage the skin or the jaw bone.

The only disadvantage of a flash noseband is that there are two nosebands cluttering up the horse's head – and too often both of them are tighter than they should be.

The Grakle Noseband

The Grakle noseband is named after the famous Grand National winner. It con-

Fig 76   A Grakle noseband fitted on an eggbutt snaffle bridle, the headpiece of which is too small – a common fault with modern, ready-made bridles.

sists of two quite narrow noseband straps which are joined where they cross over in front of the horse's face just above the muzzle. The headpiece is attached to the top loop which goes above the bit, while the lower loop passes under the bit in a similar manner to the flash noseband. It is a wise precaution to have a small pad of sheepskin attached to the front of the noseband to prevent chafing where the straps cross and are joined. The two nosebands should have a short connecting strap at the back which prevents the top strap from rising too far above the horse's mouth.

The main purpose of a Grakle noseband is to prevent the horse from crossing his jaw, pulling and even getting beyond his rider's control. It is a lightweight noseband and will often suit an impetuous Thoroughbred for work over fences or in the hunting field.

The Mexican Noseband

This is similar to the Grakle noseband, but the two loops of the cross-over noseband are positioned further apart. The headpiece is shorter and the top loop is fitted further up on the horse's cheeks, across the masseter muscles. There is no connecting strap at the back of this pattern of noseband.

The purpose of the Mexican noseband is similar to that of the Grakle; theoretically it has more subtle intentions as the higher loop is intended to have a massaging effect which eases away the unwanted constraint or excess tension in the masseter muscles, thus restoring the required compliant mobility of the lower jaw.

There are several other types of noseband, some of which seem to have worthy objectives but which, in practice, prove to have major disadvantages. All nosebands of the drop variety are used only with a snaffle bridle; they must never be used with a double bridle or a Pelham for the simple reason that the chin groove is very small. It cannot accommodate the back strap of a drop noseband as well as a curb chain; thus if the two are fitted together, the chain will be pushed up on to the sharp edges of the lower jaw which will be injured by its pinching pressure.

Conclusion

To finish on a high, yet warning, note, a quotation from the FEI dressage rule book reads:

The horse ... accepts the bridle with a light and soft contact and submissiveness throughout ... he may quietly champ the bit.

This soft 'chewing' is a desirable quality;

it must not be impaired by too tight a noseband.

I seem to have written at length on one of my least favourite subjects. I do hope that this chapter may be of assistance to riders and, through them, to their horses. I could not count how many times, when judging and teaching at home and abroad, I have been asked, 'Please would you show us how to use a chambon for lungeing and how to ride with running-reins?' As I always say that I welcome questions of any sort, what could I answer but, 'Certainly,' adding, 'if, after working your horse for twenty minutes, I find that he needs it!' As yet, I have never had to demonstrate either gadget.

Finally, it should be understood that if a trainer's horsemanship is lacking, he may have to use a gadget – that is, if he does not lunge well enough or if his riding is at fault. Every gadget used tells a tale against the trainer who uses it. The best place to keep gadgets of all sorts is in the saddler's cupboard.

11 Bitless Bridles

by Susan McBane

In the Preface, I said that the subject of bitting was as subject to fashion as any other. Bitless bridles, in particular, seem to have been going through a favoured phase for the past 10 or 15 years, particularly in showjumping. Even if you do not feel like going to the extremes of riding without a bridle at all (except for in the relatively safe confines of your own manège) as described by Moyra Williams in the next chapter, you may feel like trying bitless riding, if only out of curiosity, which was the reason I tried it some years ago.

Going Bitless

There are various reasons for going bitless. A few horses are very difficult to bit comfortably due to having some extreme mouth conformation – perhaps an unusually big tongue, exceptionally sensitive bars or back teeth placed further forward than usual (this is very rare but is not unknown). If a horse sustains a mouth injury of some kind or if a youngster's mouth is so sore during teething that he does not seem able to happily wear a bit at all, never mind accept its pressure, a bitless bridle can enable work to continue effectively, the horse to be exercised and fitness maintained.

People who have never ridden bitless are often surprised at what little difference the lack of a bit makes to the way their horse goes – in many cases there is a noticeable improvement, especially where the normal rider does not have the best of hands. This is not really surprising when we remember that most horses are lunged or long-reined at the beginning of their working life in a lungeing cavesson which, of course, has no bit. The horses are accustomed to vocal directions at this stage, and the voice continues to be used during early mounted training so that the horse comes to associate each already familiar command with the new aids given by a rider. The voice is ultimately largely dispensed with.

The horse has, by this time, become thoroughly familiar with the rider's back, seat, leg and hand aids, the latter being felt not only through the bit but on the neck, the poll, the chin groove and the nose depending on the type of bit and bridle used. Also, when open rein is used the horse can see the rider's hand moving sideways to indicate direction. Only the poorest of riders would rely almost entirely on the bit for control – and if the rider is that bad the horse would probably be only too willing to go better if the bit were dispensed with! It is, therefore, not so surprising after all that horses usually go well and willingly in bitless bridles and are not confused by the loss of direction and instruction felt through the bit.

Novice riders often ask how they are supposed to cope should the horse run away with them, failing to appreciate (perhaps because they may never have been run away with) that the mere fact of a horse's having a bit in its mouth does not prevent this. Horses are extremely strong animals who generally go along with our strange requests because of their mental willingness to co-exist, not because we have physically dominated them. Unless a horse is trussed up like a chicken ready for the oven, or physically restrained in some other inescapable way, if he takes it into his head to do something or not to do something, he can easily do it physically and the bit in his mouth may make no real difference. If the bit is used brutally, a spirited horse can easily deposit his rider in retaliation against the pain, whereas a less spirited one may react differently but just as violently out of panic and fear.

Bitless bridles do not, by any means, offer less control than those with bits. Control is, after all, achieved by communication and the horse's willingness to comply. If more than mere control is required, if the rider seeks actual collection, with its requisite flexion at the poll, again this can be obtained with some types of bitless bridle with no more difficulty than by the use of a bit or bits in the horse's mouth.

Types

Simple Noseband

Probably the simplest type of bitless bridle is a noseband made of cord or binder twine with reins of a similar material attached at each side. The nose-band will be most effective if it is fitted about four fingers' width above the nostrils, resting at the end of the face bone just before the cartilage or gristly part begins. It should be fitted closely but not tightly. Control will be entirely on the nose and by means of neck-reining.

An ordinary headcollar can be used, with reins fastened to each side D-ring, and will provide similar pressure points. Anyone who has ridden a horse to or from the field with a headcollar and rope has, in effect, ridden in a bitless bridle. More control can be obtained by passing a piece of leather or rope through both side D-rings under the jaw and joining its ends at the horse's withers. This will obviously create pressure not only on the nose but under the jaw so that there is all-round pressure.

Drop Noseband

A strong drop noseband can also be used, with the reins fastened to the side rings. A browband can be added to stop it sliding back down the neck and a throatlatch improvised with binder twine. The back-strap of the noseband should be fastened closely but not tightly, to stop it slipping around. Here, control is achieved by pressure on the nose (but not under the jaw obviously) and by neck-reining. Again, the backstrap could be removed and a length of leather or rope passed through the side rings and up to the withers, as described for the headcollar.

Scawbrig

The control achieved with the drop nose-band is just the same as with a proper Scawbrig bitless bridle. This consists of a conventional headpiece with all-in-one

111

*Fig 77   A Scawbrig bitless bridle.
Most designs have a thick, padded
section behind the jaw rather than a
single strip of leather like this. The
cheekpieces can be adjusted so that the
nosepiece is a little lower than this and
the padded section would then come in
the chin groove.*

throatlatch and cheekpieces supporting a
padded (usually chamois leather) nosepiece with strong side rings. In the chin
groove is another padded section, tapering into reins which pass through the side
rings and up to the rider's hands. Control
is achieved by all-round pressure on the
nose and jaw. An added advantage of this
bridle is that it is specifically intended to
be used in mouthing a horse, as a sliphead
can be added, if desired, to support a bit in
the horse's mouth.

At first, the bit just hangs there with no
reins, to accustom the horse to being
ridden with a bit in its mouth, but the
rider only has control through the bitless
part. This is useful with youngsters who
may throw their heads about and receive
from the rider an inadvertent jab in the
mouth if just using reins in the normal

way. Later, reins are attached to the bit so
the rider has two pairs of reins but
initially continues to ride mostly on the
'bitless' reins. Gradually, the bit is
brought more and more into use during
the youngster's schooling, but the bitless
part is still available should there be an
emergency. Finally, of course, the Scawbrig is dispensed with and the horse goes
into an ordinary bridle.

The Scawbrig was the bitless bridle I
first used out of curiosity, and I rode my
Anglo-Arab gelding in it, without the bit
attachment, for two years. It was only an
incident on Knott End Beach, when he
suddenly decided he wanted to visit
Morecambe and was heading towards the
bay's treacherous quicksands, that made
me think perhaps I should revert to being
more conventional and started using a bit
again! However, the bit made no difference as he repeated the performance three
months later. This horse had been ridden
on the beach all his working life and only
took off like that on those two occasions,
which I must now put down to incom-
petent riding on my part, being unable to
find any other excuse. Certainly, the bit
appeared to give me no more control than
a Scawbrig. The Scawbrig was subsequently used by friends on their horses,
both confirming that their horses went
just as well in it as with a bit.

Running and Draw-Reins

Running reins and draw-reins (*see* Chapter 10) can both be used with either a
plain drop noseband used as a bitless
bridle or with a Scawbrig, being passed
through the side rings instead of the bit
rings. This gives extra control, if desired
(and poll pressure in the case of draw-
reins). If a bitless bridle is being used for a

horse who has become afraid of bit pressure and has started to go with his head up and nose out in an effort to divert bit pressure from the bars to the corners of the lips, he may continue to go this way for a while in a bitless bridle out of habit. In such cases, running reins and draw-reins would both encourage him to lower his head until he gets the idea that the bit is not going to hurt him any more (because it isn't there) and realises that a lower, rounder way of going is more comfortable and efficient.

Blair's Pattern

Home-made devices consisting of head-collars and drop nosebands, and proper Scawbrig bridles are the mildest bitless bridles. The type most often seen on showjumpers, and initially brought to the general attention of the horse world by Eddie Macken and Boomerang, employ actual leverage rather than direct pressure, and can be very severe in their action. In Britain, they are incorrectly, but widely, called hackamores, but their correct name is Blair's pattern bitless bridles. They require very sensitive hand-ling and it can be said that if a rider is not competent to handle a double bridle, he cannot handle a Blair either.

A Blair, of which there are several variations all operating on the same prin-ciples, consists of an ordinary headpiece with cheekpieces and throatlatch, nose-band (usually padded), backstrap or curbstrap and a long metal cheek at each side, the actual length varying consider-ably up to about a third of a metre (a foot) or more. The cheekpieces, noseband and backstrap are attached to the metal cheeks at the top, top-front and top-back res-pectively and the reins fasten to the

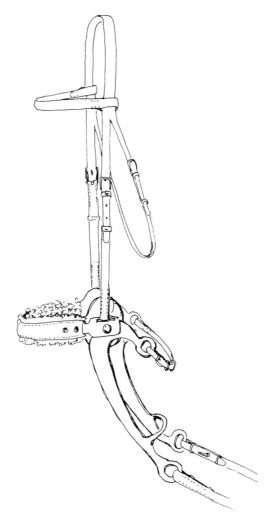

Fig 78   A Blair's pattern bitless bridle, usually incorrectly called a 'hackamore' in the UK.

bottom of each metal cheek.

Pressure on the reins results in pressure on the poll, nose and lower jaw (some-what higher than the chin groove) and can be very severe depending on the length of the cheeks (the longer they are the stronger the leverage and subsequent pressure) and the strength of the rein aid. A similar design of bridle is used in the Americas on youngsters being schooled to Western riding, where it is known as the Hackamore Bit Bridle.

The noseband and backstrap of the Blair bridle need to be fitted closely to be effective and are both usually padded or lined with sheepskin and kept in soft condition to avoid creating soreness. The cheekpieces should be adjusted regularly up and down to change the position of the noseband and backstrap to avoid callousing and loss of sensitivity. The noseband should be fitted above the ending of the nose cartilage and never less than about 7-8cm (3in) above the nostrils.

As mentioned, considerable skill and sensitivity are needed to use a Blair, especially the longer-cheeked varieties. As with a curb bit, the pressure on the reins must be very light because of the multiplying factor caused by the leverage exerted through the metal cheeks.

Jumping Hackamore

Perhaps a less skilled rider would be safer using a Scawbrig or a bridle which is now quite common on the continent of Europe but not so much in the United Kingdom, called the bitless jumping bridle or jumping hackamore. It uses direct nose pressure like the Scawbrig but is of slightly different design.

It consists of a headpiece, throatlatch and cheekpieces which fork at their ends and are attached to a stiffened, slightly padded rolled noseband. The two rear forks of the cheekpieces are joined under the lower jaw by a leather strap a little way above the chin groove. The noseband itself is open at the back, each branch having a ring to which the reins attach. Direct rein action results in pressure on the nose – raising the hand tilts the noseband downwards slightly and causes slight pressure under the lower jaw.

WS Bitless Pelham

The Distas Pelham, often described in old books and now known more commonly as the WS Bitless Pelham, offers more versatility as it is used with two pairs of reins – the snaffle reins which exert direct pressure, and the 'curb' reins which employ leverage on the chin groove by means of a conventional curb chain. It consists of a padded nosebar or strap on two short metal bars. These short bars are joined to two metal cheeks which curve backwards at the top and end in hooks to which the curb chain fits. The pair of eyes near the joint take the snaffle reins and the rings at the bottom of the cheeks take the curb reins. As each cheek can also move independently of its partner, a good deal of precision is possible.

Hackamore

The hackamore proper is essentially an item of Western riding equipment, and consists of a heavy, plaited rawhide nosepiece known as a bosal, with a heavy knot (the heel knot) to balance it under the jaw (the weight of both the bosal and the heel knot lessen as the horse advances in training). It is kept in place by a light headstall (*latigo*) which is usually split to pass over one ear, although sometimes a browband (*cavesada*) is added for extra security. A throatlatch (*fiador*) is often added. This is a light cotton or horse hair rope fastened round the throat, knotting under it and attaching to the heel knot to

Fig 79   A true Western hackamore.

finesse and control can be achieved without a bit as with one. Highly-trained hackamore horses are capable of performing the most intricate movements at full speed on what appears to be the weight of the rein and with perfect balance – no mean feat whatever school of equitation you belong to.

As with the Scawbrig, the hackamore can be, and is commonly, used to accustom the horse to being ridden and to take him to a high standard of training before the introduction of the bit – in the case of Western riding a curb bit. This is added and ultimately takes over, the final object being a horse who goes on the floating weight of a quarter-inch rawhide rein.

prevent it banging about on the lower jaw. Cotton, wool or horse-hair reins (*mecate*) attach to the heel knot and rear branches of the bosal by wrapping round them. By this means, the 'lie' of the bosal on the head can be finely adjusted and balanced. It is brought into use on the nose by the rider lifting his hand. When not in use it is so well balanced that it barely touches the head. The noseband lies a good 10cm (4in) above the nostrils. The rear shanks of the bosal do not normally touch the horse's lower jaw.

However, if a more closely fitting bosal is purposely used, this does work on the branches of the lower jaw, which are more sensitive than the nose. This results in a flexed, high-headed way of going with considerable weight on the hocks – it calls for a highly sensitive and competent rider.

With either fitting of bosal, the true hackamore bridle, probably of all the bitless bridles available, is the one to convince bit devotees that just as much

Training

Adjusting to riding in a bitless bridle involves no great effort on the part of the rider. There is no magic to it, but those who are rather 'bit orientated' would probably benefit from learning to ride more with their seat, weight, balance and legs than relying on their hands and what they have perhaps hitherto considered the 'indispensable' bit. This is particularly important with the more severe types of bitless bridle such as the Blair. Horses who have been used to a fairly significant and constant bit contact also adjust quite quickly to having no bit and often go more willingly. Even in a bitless bridle, if you pull, he'll pull too. That principle does not change!

You could begin by walking circles, concentrating on relaxing your seat and legs, and feeling the horse's back through your seat (perhaps on the lunge if you have someone who will lunge you). Keep a light contact on the reins, particularly if using a Blair, and practise slowing and speeding up by means of half halts. Take your shoulders back a little, give a slight push under with your seatbones and take in the reins slightly (not a backward pull). Conversely, give a little with the reins as you push with your seat and give an aid with your leg to increase speed. Remember to use your voice, too. Your horse well remembers the commands taught to him on the lunge and you can use them now to reinforce your body aids.

Progress to figure-eights and simple school figures in walk, then in trot, using the same principles to speed up and slow down within a gait, and from walk to trot and vice versa. Keep the horse listening to you by means of frequent changes of direction, but warn him of your intentions in plenty of time by means of slight half halts and changes of body position.

By the time you canter the horse will be getting the hang of more body and less hand, if it is new to him, and is unlikely to give you trouble. You can progress to jumping at home and do things as gradually as you like, but this transition period will probably be more for your benefit than the horse's.

It is largely a case of acquiring a truly independent seat and thinking more in terms of body and legs rather than as much hand as you have perhaps been accustomed to using in the past. Having no bit, certainly, is not an excuse to feel free and easy with the reins and use them to keep yourself on without fear of socking the horse in the mouth (although bitless bridles of the milder type, without leverage, are a boon for novice riders and their teachers, not to mention their horses).

For true harmony and control, an independent seat and the knowledge of how to use it is what to aim for – and can only benefit your ability and the horse's comfort, with or without a bit.

12 Look – No Bridle!

by Moyra Williams, PhD

The necessity of having a bit in a horse's mouth in order to control it has been doubted by many people over the years. The ancient Arabs, it is said, controlled their magnificent steeds – or at least directed them – by means of light lengths of cotton flapping round their necks. The North American Indians used leather thongs in a similar manner, and some of the Egyptian frescos show teams of horses ploughing and pulling carts with no form of harness on their heads at all.

We do not have to go back in history to find horses that are directed by unconventional methods. Some circus trainers admit that the end of a whip or the position of a handkerchief is often used to tell horses when to stand up or turn round. Even in conventional sports these days there are some riders who prefer the hackamore (a bitless bridle with long cheekpieces to which the reins are attached) to other forms of bridle.

I entered this field by a very different route. During the first few years after the Second World War, traditional equestrian sports, while struggling back on to their feet, offered a great welcome to anyone who wished to join in, and show-jumping seemed to many to offer a great opportunity and challenge. Showjumping had up till then been a largely professional affair, organised and carried out by a small group of showmen who toured the agricultural shows throughout the summer, drawing in audiences by their feats of daring. They competed for paltry sums of money over enormous, brightly-coloured obstacles. To their credit, these old stalwarts welcomed competition from the ambitious amateurs who came to join them and never stinted in offering advice and encouragement.

But advice is one thing; acquiring the skill to take them on at their own game was another. Show jumps, in those days, were mainly straight, perpendicular obstacles built from poles laid one above the other. They were measured entirely by the height of the topmost pole, which had to be jumped clean, for the slightest brush would remove a light wooden slat laid on top of it, incurring half a penalty.

The secret of success was for the horse to be able to round its back when jumping, and flick its hind feet up over its head before coming down – a manoeuvre which involved keeping its head low and its quarters well underneath it when approaching the fence. This manoeuvre is, in fact, just what the cow-cutting ponies of the USA use to achieve incredible feats of speed and agility without any interference from the rider. (In fact, if a rider is seen to give his horse any touch after showing it the selected calf, he loses points.)

117

First Experiments

It was while watching such a cow-cutting performance from the top of a stand on the West Coast of the USA that an idea began to take shape in my mind. If I could guide and control a horse without interfering with its head at all – in other words leaving it entirely free to use its head and neck as balancing poles – what heights of success could we achieve in the show-jumping world? Would it be possible for any horse to beat us? There was just one small problem, however, in that horses had not only to be able to clear those fences in the show ring, they had to jump them in the right order and within a certain time limit, and often this involved complicated and unexpected turns, or sudden stops followed immediately by acceleration in a different direction. Speed and accuracy were central to a good score. And finally there was another not inconsiderable problem of the rider having to control and deliver his signals to the horse from a position on its back. The techniques used by circus trainers were thereby eliminated.

As it happened, I had at about that time been involved in some work comparing the sensitivity of the skin over different parts of the horse's body and in horses of different coat colours, and it had become apparent that the area of the neck in front and to the side of the withers was, in all the horses we had tried, particularly sensitive to the touch of the human hand. It occurred to me that if signals were to be given by a rider on parts of the horse other than the sides of the mouth (by the bit) or on the flanks (by the leg) then touch with the fingers on the sides of the withers would be the ideal area to make for. A sharp backward scrape with both hands could signal stop (or slow down), a sharp forward thrust the opposite (go, or faster) and a push on either side could mean turn away. At any rate, the prospect seemed worth trying out, so as soon as I returned to England, I set about acquiring a horse on which to test the possibility.

To avoid the necessity of having to supplant one set of learned habits by another, I decided to start on a young, unbroken horse and teach it my neck aids from the very beginning. My choice fell – perhaps not too wisely – on a very beautiful but extremely spoilt and highly-strung three-quarter Thoroughbred filly whose one idea of fun turned out to be to disobey every command of her rider or handler; and if loose in the field, cause the maximum possible disturbance and chaos among her equine companions. She very soon introduced me to the grave and previously unconsidered problem of ensuring her obedience to the signals.

Even with the conventional tack, this is a problem. There is no way, short of complete confinement, that obedience to a signal can be enforced; and all a rider can ever do really is convince his mount that it is in its own best interests to do what is asked of it. However, by dint of accompanying my signals with gentle physical pressure in the early stages (a pull on the head-collar to stop or turn; someone pushing her back end to go forward) we began to make progress; and to my great satisfaction and delight it did not really take her longer to learn these signals than it usually took me to break a horse to the conventional aids. Even when simple flat work was combined with elementary jumping, the signals were obeyed without too much demur.

I then faced the all-important question

of what would happen in a strange environment. Would my bitless horse be as controllable in public as a fully kitted one? Or would the last anyone saw of me be a disappearing backside sinking over a distant horizon? And this is where I personally had my greatest surprise and satisfaction from the whole experiment. In strange surroundings, the horse was *more* alert to my signals, *more* obedient to a command, and more amenable to my desires than she ever had been at home. It seemed as though – and this is only common sense when you think about it – whereas in her home territory she knew what to expect and what she could get away with, in strange surroundings *I* was her only link with security, and it was on me she depended for her safety.

Portia

Whether this particular mare would ever have fulfilled my ambition of becoming a leading showjumper we will never know as she had barely been in my possession six months when fate struck a cruel blow and dealt her a fatal dose of colic. Fortunately, however, her successor – a chestnut half Irish Draught filly called Portia who I bought as a replacement – although even less promising at first appearances, turned out to fulfil all my dreams and ambitions, and became a legend in her time for her accuracy, quickness on the turn and docile obedience in public. Her successes as a showjumper were numerous, despite my own limited opportunities for competing, and were only exceeded by the eulogies (or ribald remarks!) she received over the loudspeakers from the commentators who were just beginning to make a

considerable impact on the sport.

I was not entirely amused by one, however, who, just as I was about to jump a fence, came over the loud-speaker with the remark, 'You will see Mrs Williams has nothing on ...,' and as I landed the other side, continued, '... her horse's head'. The roar of laughter from the audience put paid to any further serious activity on our part that day.

However, riding in an arena – even a large outdoor one – is not quite the same as riding across country, and this was something I also had to try. Like her predecessor, Portia was obedience itself in new or open territory, but after I had been out cubbing on her several times I could not help wondering what might happen if, while we were galloping in full flight across a field, we suddenly had to put on the brakes. Unforgettable visions came to my mind of the pack losing the scent and spreading out to cast, with Portia and I careering through the middle of it and an infuriated Master and huntsmen swearing at our backs. When the moment actually came, however, how stupid and ungrounded all those nightmares seemed! Portia was the first horse among the charging mass which seemed to realise and respond to the sudden absence of 'music' from the pack ahead, and on went her brakes. To his credit, the Master (who did not exactly approve of my antics) was the first to comment on his surprise.

Nor was this the only time I found I had misjudged the mare's sagacity. If, at the end of a day, I was uncertain as to the best way home or where I had left my transport, I found I had only to leave the matter to Portia. It soon became apparent that she was not only alert to these environmental signs, but that she was

119

*Fig 80 Unfortunately, no photographs survive of Portia jump-
ing 'with nothing on' but this photograph shows her and the
author of this chaper in a bitless bridle with reins flapping, a
way in which they sometimes competed. No pressure was
exerted on the bridle at all, either between the jumps or over
them.*

also responding to all sorts of other signs
and signals from me, many of which I had
not realised – or intended – giving. Self
doubts (perhaps shown by the tremor of
a finger), exhaustion (floppiness in the
saddle?), fear (half-heartedness in my
signal to go forward?) and many, many
other signals were picked up by her and
responded to – as, indeed, I am sure all
horses pick up and respond to such
signals even when ridden in the conventional tack.

My efforts at point-to-pointing Portia
were less successful because of the absence, in those days, of a breastplate
which would keep the saddle in place
without the necessity for a strap over the
withers; and as she became racing fit and
lost her naturally large stomach there was
a tendency for the saddle to slip back.
Schooling over short distances up on the
Wantage Downs was no problem, and
the trainer who kindly provided the
facilities and companions for me to do so
quickly overcame his initial apprehen-
sions at a bridle-less horse flying along

with his precious charges. But, three fences out on our first race, I found myself sliding back towards Portia's tail – and on over her side under her stomach.

Other competitions, such as dressage and combined training, were barred to us because the 'rules' insist on horses being ridden in specified bridles; and even though we showed we could carry out the required movements, the governing bodies were reluctant to alter their regulations for us. Our final outing together was a long-distance trip to completely new territory in Devon, which I undertook to see if Portia would be able to find her way back to our Oxfordshire base unguided. Whether she would indeed have been able to, however, I never did discover, as she seemed to think Devon would be a lovely place to settle down in, and was perfectly content to stand by the roadside for day after day eating the lush grass until I gave up.

I have to admit that riding without bit or bridle did present certain problems. There was the matter of controlling the horse when not on its back – a problem I solved by keeping a head-collar on Portia while away from home, with reins loosely attached to the sides which could be thrown over her head and held to one side. There was also the question of what to do with, and where to put, my hands when they were not giving signals. All too often, I would leave them resting loosely on her neck, gradually becoming aware of Portia's puzzlement as she tried to interpret what I was saying! More serious still was the danger of inadvertently pushing them down on to her withers in order to keep myself in the saddle if I lost my balance, so signalling her to leap forward when what I really wanted to do was stop. This would have been fatal, as the essence of any form of signal for it to be effective is *consistency* – just as the essence of true communication is being prepared to receive as well as transmit messages.

If a particularly firm and well-balanced seat is necessary in order to be able to give consistent messages on the neck, then clearly it is not a system to recommend to novice riders; and this is what eventually led me to abandon the technique or recommend it to others. Besides that, having a universal set of aids (using whatever technique is fashionable) which is used by everyone in all countries, has the advantage that riders and horses can be interchanged without causing confusion.

13 Bitting for the Major Sports

Dressage

by Jennie Loriston-Clarke,
MBE, FBHS

When riding in dressage competitions there are two types of bit allowed, either snaffle bits or the bridoon and curb bits which make up the double bridle.

The Snaffle

The snaffle bit is the foundation bit in which the horse does all his early training, and should be made of metal with one or two joints. A straight bar or mullen mouth is also acceptable, and there are also different synthetic materials, such as rubber and nylon, which are permitted. I would shy away from using these, however, as when you get higher up the ladder only metal snaffles (or bridoons, as they are called) are allowed when using a double bridle.

The jointed snaffle bit acts on the horse's tongue, bars and corners of the mouth, but we should not talk about the bit alone, because it quickly becomes an instrument of restraint and torture in the wrong hands. The bit is used in conjunction with the rider's seat, legs and hands, which through the reins take up the control and balance of the horse. The correct choice of bit is basically what suits the horse. I find most horses go kindly in a lightweight loose-ring snaffle, as the mouthpiece is thick and comfortable for the horse to take a light contact. But take care that the corners of the lips do not get pinched between the bit ring and the mouthpiece.

Some horses prefer the double jointed action of the French Link. This folds round the tongue and has a little more action on the bars of the mouth. Some people prefer to train their horses in an eggbutt bridoon, as they do not then have to change the snaffle bit at all when transferring to the double bridle. This is often a help and prevents too many changes for the horse.

When starting a young horse it may be helpful to use a cheek snaffle to aid turning, as this prevents the bit pulling through the mouth. All this, however, should be preceded by careful examination of the horse's mouth and teeth. Wolf teeth can cause a lot of pain and discomfort in the horse as they have small roots and are apt to move should the bit touch them. The riding horse's mouth should be checked for sharp molars every six months and these rasped so that the cheeks are not chafed by the action of the bit or noseband.

The horse wears a snaffle bit during training, and some time must be taken to see what type of snaffle the horse will accept. 'Accepting the bit' means that the horse is happy for you to take a light contact on the reins, having preceded this

Fig 81   A French link snaffle.

with closure of the legs and seat to push the horse's energy into the hand so that balance and steering can be initiated. When the horse 'accepts the bit' it relaxes its lower jaw, and its head and neck is placed in a correct outline for the pace it is performing. The mouth should be wet with saliva and the horse attentive.

The snaffle bit used must fit the horse's mouth. It must be wide enough, but must not be more than half an inch wider than the jaw. If the bit is too wide it will pull through the mouth and the joint could damage the bars of the mouth. If the horse is inclined to lean on the bit it may be advisable to ride with a finer mouthpiece. A horse which is inclined to shy away from the contact is helped with a thick mouthpiece. Some horses take a steadier contact if the bit is fairly heavy and thick and others prefer the lightweight hollow stainless steel bit. I was always taught it was the hands which made a horse's mouth. Unsteady rough hands make a horse resist and stiffen its neck and lower jaw; in this case it will be unresponsive and slow to react to the rider's wishes.

The Double Bridle

The rider must be able to perform all the transitions happily in a snaffle before progressing to a double bridle. The double bridle is made up of a bridoon, which is a smaller ringed snaffle with a single or double joint, and a Weymouth or curb bit with a curb chain. Each bit works independently, with the Weymouth being used as a refinement of the snaffle. The Weymouth bit acts on the bars of the mouth, the poll and the curb groove, with a little tongue pressure depending on the port of the mouthpiece. The length of the cheek both above and below the mouthpiece relates to the severity of the bit. The longer the distance above the mouthpiece the greater the leverage on the poll and curb groove. The cheek below the mouthpiece is usually one and a half times that above – anything longer is considered a long cheek. A bit with a very short distance between both is called a Tom Thumb and is the mildest type of curb bit.

When adjusting the bits in the horse's mouth care must be taken that not only do they fit correctly but also that they hang in the correct position. The bridoon should lie just above the Weymouth when there is a light contact taken up. The Weymouth should be adjusted comfortably just below the bridoon or just above the tush of the upper jaw, if the horse has one. The curb chain should be turned in a clockwise direction until it is smooth and looped on to the curb hooks so that when the contact is taken up the angle of the cheeks does not exceed 45 degrees to the horse's lips.

There are Weymouths with fixed

cheeks and sliding cheeks. In dressage the fixed cheek is used most commonly as riders do not like the horse playing with its tongue too much (*see* Chapter 7). The sliding cheek Weymouth is designed to encourage the horse to use its tongue and to play with the bit which helps to make it salivate. This bit is useful for a horse with a dry mouth and also a horse which leans on the bit. The fixed cheek Weymouth has many different thicknesses of mouth-piece and height of port. The Weymouth puts most pressure on the bars of the mouth and, depending on the height of the port, a little pressure on the tongue. Some horses dislike pressure on the ton-gue and in this case the Schultheiss Wey-mouth is a good bit as it gives the tongue plenty of room and has a thick mouth-piece which is not too sharp for the horse. For a horse which likes some tongue pressure the mullen mouth Weymouth is useful and many horses go kindly in it.

When riding dressage, many riders like

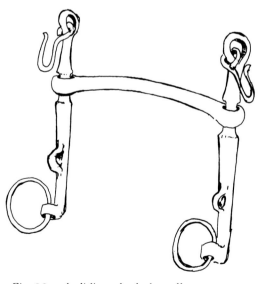

Fig 82 A sliding cheeked, mullen mouthed Weymouth.

to warm the horse up in its snaffle bit and then change into the double bridle for the last ten minutes. On the whole, if the horse is correctly trained it should be confident in its basic snaffle, and the same should apply to the double bridle. Con-stant changes are a sign of a horse which is unhappy in its mouth, in which case I would check for sharp teeth, check my training methods and check my hands. If it was the latter perhaps a few lessons would not go amiss!

Eventing

by Jane Holderness-Roddam

Eventing is a demanding sport and requires an extremely versatile horse. It must perform a dressage test in a relaxed and calm way, correctly moving forward between hand and leg. On the cross country it must gallop over solid fences and be controllable enough to cope with some of the most awkward of fences, possibly going up or down hill over them. For the showjumping the horse must be sufficiently obedient to be able to jump neatly and cleanly round a set course of coloured fences.

To do all this successfully it is obvious-ly most important that the right bit is used to ensure a sufficient degree of control for each section. In the dressage phase there are certain rules laid down for the different levels determining what types of bit are allowed. At novice level only a snaffle bridle may be used. The different types permitted are clearly laid down in the dressage rule book or by the FEI, but include snaffles with single or double jointed mouthpieces (although Dr Bristol bits are excluded). Unjointed bits and those with or without cheekpieces are all allowed, as are bits made of rubber, vulcanite or nylon, but all must be in their original manufactured state with no other additions.

For intermediate and advanced standard tests the double bridle may be used. The bits allowed on a double are again confined to those illustrated in the rule books. The bridoon may be single or double jointed and various types of curb are allowed. Curb chains may be single or double linked and have a rubber or leather cover.

For any bit to be comfortable the horse must have a healthy mouth. Regular rasping by a vet may not be enough as few vets understand the action of the bit and noseband and tend to rasp purely to improve the horse's ability to masticate rather than checking for hooks that are rough on the insides and outsides of the teeth. A specialist horse dentist may be advisable if you feel your horse is unhappy in its mouth. Check also for wolf teeth, as these are a very common cause of discomfort. The width and thickness of the bit can affect many horses. If a bit is too wide for the mouth the direct action effect will be lost. If it is too narrow it will pinch and cut into the cheeks. Mouth ulcers, sores and splits in the lip will all contribute to fussiness and head shaking so do check that all is well in that direction before wondering what else is affecting the horse. Study your horse's mouth – is it small or large, and does a certain bit seem too thick? Some horses cannot tolerate the nutcracker action of the jointed bit and seem much happier in a straight or half moon bit.

The action of the bit can be considerably influenced by the type of noseband used and while only a cavesson can be used with the double bridle, drops, flashes and the Grakle are allowed with a snaffle at any level (*see* Chapter 10). These may be particularly helpful with horses that tend to open their mouths or cross their jaws but don't forget that they will make the action of the bit more severe, so stronger leg and a lighter hand may be required.

Cross Country

For the cross country phase control is essential, and while the majority of horses go in a snaffle perhaps with the addition of a running martingale for greater steerage, some horses require something stronger. It must be remembered, however, that, particularly in the cross country phase, horse and rider are inevitably not always going to be in complete harmony over every type of fence. While the more experienced rider may be able to compensate for this by slipping the reins, giving the horse the freedom over the fence that it requires, other riders often catch their horses in the mouth as they lose balance. A horse will not jump anything well if this happens too often as it will start to associate the pain of this with jumping a fence and soon compensate by throwing its head up and dropping its hind legs in an effort to avoid this unhappy situation, or will stop altogether.

The old saying 'if you don't pull at him, he won't pull at you' is very true in most cases and is always worth bearing in mind, but in the excitement of the competitive atmosphere the majority of horses will pull harder and may become too strong to be safely ridden round a tough cross country course.

Snaffles The various types of roller snaffle are meant to prevent the horse leaning on the bit. Its action is accentuated by the type of noseband used depending on whether the horse tends to open its mouth or cross its jaw. The square mouthpiece of the Cornish (or Scorrier) snaffle, with two rings either side, keeps the bit higher in the mouth and is another very effective bit in which many horses seem to go kindly.

The Kineton noseband with a snaffle may make an enormous difference to some horses. Its action on the nose and its effect of keeping the bit forward in the mouth, so reducing tongue pressure and causing less action on the lips and corners of the mouth, suits many horses.

D-Rings For horses that don't turn very well, a D-ring or cheeked snaffle may help especially if used with a running martingale and flash or Grakle noseband. Bad cases may be better with a brush rather than a more severe bit.

Gags The gag is a very useful bit for cross country but in the wrong unsympathetic hands its action can be horrific. When using this bit it is so important to remember that it works by pressure on the poll, mouth and tongue in particular and has a raising effect. So often it is seen used with a running martingale which is far too tight. This combination is designed to lower the head and therefore totally contradicts itself. I believe gags should only be used by themselves, and the riders must understand that a pull and release action on the reins is necessary for the bit to work properly. The bit pulls up in the mouth and down on the poll when used, and to keep pulling will prevent there being a reaction unless the rein is released a little and taken up again. There is a variety of gags on the market and rubber covered ones are often all that is required. For very strong horses the cherry roller is particularly effective. Because of its severity, I believe cavesson nosebands are the best to use with this bit. Some opening of the mouth is likely and total restriction of this could cause a sudden reaction which is not ideal when going across country.

Curb bits Curb bits are sometimes used across country. These are generally disliked by most riders because they may involve two reins, which can be muddling, and when things go wrong their action is very severe. However, for horses that go with their heads too high, the Pelham may be the answer. Many horses also go very kindly in a Kimblewick, which has less of a lowering action, only one rein and is just a little stronger than many snaffles. The double bridle is extremely versatile and in the right hands, used by those who fully understand the action of the two bits, it is highly effective but considered by most people to be rather too complicated in the heat of the cross country phase.

Fig 83   A Cornish or Scorrier snaffle.

Bitless Bridles   Bitless bridles in my opinion are rarely suitable for the cross country but many riders have used them successfully for showjumping. They can also be very useful for schooling or if the horse gets a sore mouth, which is a problem with hard pullers.

For any bit to be successful it is very important that the horse's temperament and character are taken into account as well as the age, temperament and experience of the rider. No bit in the wrong hands will work unless the rider makes the effort to approach the problem sympathetically. The horse's mouth is very sensitive and, whether it is over-excitement, enthusiasm, greenness or lack of physical strength on the horse's part which is causing a problem, careful consideration should always be given if a stronger bit is being contemplated, as it is the hands on the end of the reins which will ultimately control the situation.

Bits for Harness Horses

by Tom Coombs

Coachmanship is a craft which must be practised at something of a distance because drivers sit farther away from their horses than riders. The voice is an essential aid which evokes instant response from intelligent horses, and the whip, as an extension of the driver's arm, can be used to calm or coerce with an inevitable time lag. The only constant contact which a driver has with his horses is through the bits in their mouths and this must be maintained through 12ft of rein with a single horse or a pair and 24ft of rein with a tandem or team.

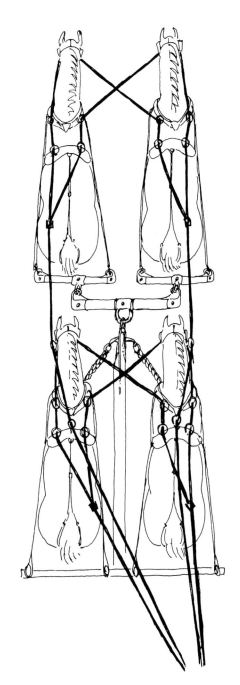

Fig 84   The coupling arrangement for the reins of a four-in-hand.

127

This rather remote control is further deflected in the case of a pair or four in hand by the arrangement which couples the reins together so that only one left rein and one right rein for each pair of horses finally reaches the driver's hand. This provision is a practical necessity to make accurate rein handling possible but it does not allow for constant even contact to be maintained with each horse's mouth. To compensate for uneven contact the coupling reins, which cross each other between the two horses, are adjustable as to the point at which they are buckled to the draft or outside reins, and there are up to five different positions at which the reins may be buckled on to the bits to vary the severity of each one's action.

Jointed Snaffles

The first bit ever known was the jointed snaffle. Invented by Sumerian charioteers five thousand years ago, it has stood the test of time and is still used by most riders and many drivers throughout the world, and all drivers in Hungary. In the seventeenth century the Hungarians added two extra rings, buckled to the cheekpieces of their bridles, through which the mouthpieces of their snaffles were suspended. This enabled them to vary the severity of the nutcracker action on the bars of their horses' mouths, as well as the port action on the roofs of them, by buckling the rein billets either through both rings on each side or just through the outside or 'floating' rings. All modern driving snaffles are double ringed. In Hungary they are sometimes called Persian snaffles in deference to their origin, but in Britain they are incongruously known as Wilson snaffles. Hungarian

driving snaffles are usually brass plated and have pierced and decorated rings to match the harness buckles. The action of a jointed snaffle on the mouth of a horse in harness induces a high head carriage and a tendency to 'star gaze'. This is traditionally acceptable in an Austro-Hungarian 'Jucker' turn-out and the present-day success of Hungarians in driving trials proves that it does not adversely affect performance.

Curb Bits

All other driving bits are of the Weymouth or Pelham type and incorporate curb action. Their mouthpieces can be of almost any shape or pattern, as for riding bits, with ports, tongue grids, or even Mohawk attachments, although drivers generally have less fanciful ideas about these than riders. The cheeks of driving bits display a wider variety of shape and design than those of riding bits and they all have at least three differently positioned rings or slots on each cheek, through which the billets of the reins may be buckled to provide greater or less leverage and thus more or less severe curb action. With the reins in the top position through the ring of the bit, which is known as 'smooth cheek', the curb chain does not operate and the effect is that of a plain bar snaffle. With the reins attached to the bottom of the cheeks, known as 'bottom bar', the curb action is equivalent to that of a long cheeked double bridle. Since the use of double reins is virtually unheard of in driving, and would be a practical impossibility except with a single horse, the precise positioning of reins on bits is a matter of critical judgement. All driving bits can be made with sliding mouthpieces and swivelling cheeks, but these refinements are insignificant at the end of driving reins. The oblique line of coupling reins can cause swivelling cheeks to press uncomfortably on the muzzles of horses in pair harness, so that bits with fixed mouthpieces, though surprisingly more difficult to acquire, are more generally useful for driving.

Buxton The Buxton bit, of English origin, with its elegantly curved cheeks joined at the bottom by a curved bar, is the parade bit *par excellence* and is used for all ceremonial and highly formal occasions throughout the world. It has three positions for the reins. The curved bottom bar is an integral part of the Buxton bit but it may be fitted, curved or

straight, to all other driving bits to link the ends of their cheeks. This is customary with a pair or team harness to prevent the cheeks of the bits interfering with the coupling reins.

Liverpool The Liverpool bit, also English, has cheeks which form complete circles round the ends of its mouthpiece, with straight, flat bars projecting below them. It provides two rein fixing positions within the rings: 'smooth cheek' round the ring itself, and 'rough cheek' round the branch of the bit within the ring below the mouthpiece, as well as two or three rein slots in the projecting bars themselves. It is probably the most widely used driving bit in the world, particularly for single harness, and is sometimes

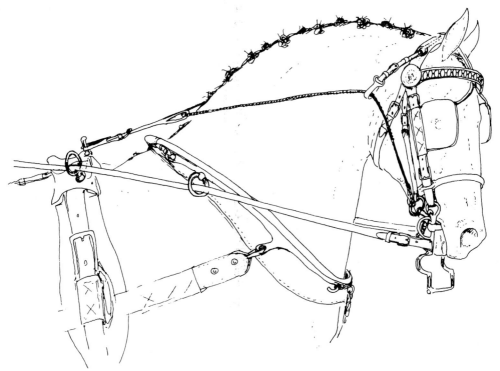

Fig 85   A Buxton bit.

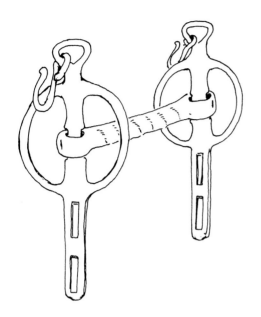

Fig 86   A Liverpool bit.

known as a Manchester bit when it has a fixed mullen mouthpiece, although this is an esoteric distinction.

Gig   The Gig bit is like the Liverpool bit but has conventional rings positioned behind the mouthpiece, as those of a Pelham. Flat, straight bars below the mouthpiece provide two or three rein slots in addition to the 'smooth cheek' but it has no 'rough cheek' position. The Tilbury bit is, in effect, a Gig bit with rigid rings projecting to the rear of round bars instead of slots in flat bars for the rein positions.

Elbow   The Elbow bit, identical to the British army port-mouthed reversible bit, has flat straight bars with rein slots set back at right angles behind the rings of the mouthpieces and projecting below them. This arrangement is intended to prevent horses catching hold of the bars

or rein billets with their teeth. A versatile bit often used with road coach harness, it is sometimes called an Ashleigh bit when it incorporates an extra rein slot just below the ring and above the elbow, which provides a position equivalent to 'rough cheek' on a Liverpool bit.

Post   The Post bit has oval shaped rings set at an angle of 45 degrees to its mouthpiece, with two or three identical rings rigidly fixed to each other at the same angle to form its extended cheeks or bars. Normally seen only on the Continent, where it is used extensively, it is a practical bit of elegant appearance to which the reins may be buckled very quickly in any of three or four different positions, hence the derivation of its name.

Bearing Reins   Bearing reins, or top reins as they are colloquially but more descriptively called, must be attached to bridoons, which for driving are lighter and have smaller rings than those used with double bridles for riding. It is wrong to attach bearing reins to curb bits since this pulls them up into the corners of horses' mouths and interferes uncomfortably with the curb action and the driver's contact with his horses' mouths. Bearing reins, which are made of cord or rounded leather, run from the bridoon rings, through rings or small pulleys on each side of the headpiece of the bridle just below the horse's ears, join together over the withers and are finally fastened to a hook or stud on the pad or saddle. Their action, on their separate bridoons, is similar to that of the top rein of a rider's double bridle in establishing and maintaining a correct head carriage, which is intentionally slightly higher for a harness horse than for a ridden horse. Contrary to popular belief, they are in no way cruel when used on horses pulling light carriages for park or show ring driving in which they do not need to lower their heads to use their weight to pull heavy loads. Bearing reins are normally used on hackneys in the show ring and they make most four in hands lighter and pleasanter for park driving by discouraging any of the horses from boring and getting over the bit.

Driving bridoons incorporating pulleys instead of rings are sometimes seen. Bearing reins pass through these pulleys and are fastened to small buckles on the bridle headpiece just below the bearing rein rings, but there is no real advantage to be gained from this extra complication. In America, roadsters and horses in fine harness classes are often shown wearing a Kimble Jackson overcheck or overdraw. This performs the same function as a bearing rein but passes over the horse's head between his ears and is attached to the same snaffle bit to which the driving reins are buckled. This apparatus tends to induce 'star gazing' by English standards but this is not objected to for the turnouts in question.

There is said to be a key to every horse's mouth and there are plenty of them available in terms of driving bits. However, the coachman himself is still the key factor in the production of a horse which is light and pleasant to drive in harness.

Long Distance and Endurance Riding

by Ann Hyland

In some equestrian disciplines and show classes there are rules as to how a horse should be bitted. In endurance riding the only requirement is that whatever restraint is used must be humane. The most common restraints are the simple jointed snaffle, Western curb and the mechanical hackamore.

The manner in which an endurance horse travels is very different, in that it proceeds forward without obvious bit restraint. The communication between horse and rider is suggested, and the horse travels with complete freedom of head and neck. That is the epitome of the *good* endurance horse. Riders of such horses are not in need of guidance as to how best to bit their mounts. They have already cracked the problem, securing that rapport which includes control and well balanced performance. Others should aim to emulate them!

Jointed Snaffle

The simple jointed snaffle would at first glance appear to be the best to use as it is the most common choice. Many horses are described as having 'a snaffle mouth'. The actuality belies the promise and the 'snaffle mouth' often turns out to be an unresponsive piece of the horse's anatomy by which the rider frequently has less control than is desired. 'Snaffle mouth' often means the horse merely wears a snaffle bit and the rider has to exert considerable and continual pressure on the horse's mouth. This is erroneously

131

phrased as 'being on the bit'.

Unfortunately, when the snaffle bit proves ineffectual it is often replaced with a mild mouthed Pelham or occasionally a Western curb. It is considered, particularly in Britain, to be bad horsemanship, uncouth on the rider's part as well as inconsiderate of him, to remind the horse that it is supposed to listen to the aid delivered via the bit, so the process repeats itself. The results are not pleasant. The horse is described as 'hard to hold' or 'a puller'. With these situations go other undesirable traits. The horse is frequently on the forehand, the forelimbs taking excess stress, the rider bearing the horse's weight via the hands, whilst the horse's hindquarters trail rather than being used for correct propulsion. This is disastrous, as one of the first lessons an endurance partnership should learn is how to conserve energy and lessen stress whilst using themselves efficiently. The rider cannot do this if he is waging a constant battle for a degree of control, or worrying about keeping the horse from tripping over if the reins should suddenly be relaxed. The horse will not be travelling economically if it is on the forehand and wasting energy fighting bit restraint.

Use a snaffle if the horse responds well – by that I mean that it should obey the lightest indication of applied pressure on the bit. If it does, it could well be bitted very mildly with a nylon mullen mouth snaffle with pinch-free eggbutt sides. It is very rare to find such an animal, however, and I have only twice been able to bit endurance horses in this way – one an Arabian stallion in America and the other Nizzolan who was very confident, well balanced and seemed to have telepathic communication, so we decided together which was the best gait.

Future patterns are set in early training. You will determine the bit to be used, and whether you have that gift of good hands, the ability when in rough country to depend on your own riding and the horse's surefootedness, and consequently the skill to leave the horse's head alone. Take the time to consider these factors. Cultivate good hands and a style of riding free from hesitancy or clutching. Make sure the horse has a good education over all types of going. Insist that it listens to you *immediately* you request its attention. Do not make repeated and stronger demands via your hands.

Most horses initially work in a snaffle, and quickly learn to ignore it. I have found that transferring a horse as quickly as possible out of a snaffle into a loose-jawed Pelham (or similar actioned Western four rein slot training bit) the best answer. The loose-jawed variety permits far more subtle bit usage. Provided your

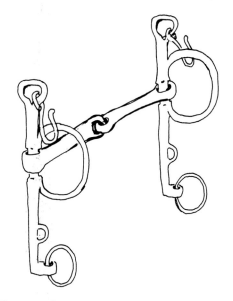

Fig 87   A jointed, sliding cheek (loose jawed) Pelham.

hands are sensitive, a sharp usage – that is, not a rough, but a quick, light, and positive use of the curb – will bring the horse to attention. It will listen and be able to be directed at the rider's wishes, rather than when it has wound down from repeated dull draggings on its mouth. These serve to gradually toughen and bruise the corners and bars of its mouth. It is *very important* that the sharp pressure is released once the response is elicited. That is the reward for compliance. The horse can then keep its mind on its work, not enter into a drawn out battle as to who pulls the hardest.

A running martingale helps with a horse that tries avoiding the bit by raising its head. It alleviates pressure on the mouth, and aids control and quicker responses because the avoidance tricks cannot be employed. When a horse has its head too high it is more likely to stumble. In endurance riding a stumble often means subsequent lameness, even if at that instant it seems none the worse for it.

Western Curb

For riders who choose a Western curb, use a moderate shank and ensure the curb strap is correctly adjusted – you need instant recall, not an ineffective bit. With a Western bit the horse must be trained to neck-rein, as turning action via the bit is almost non-existent. I feel all endurance horses should be taught to neck-rein well as they will travel better with fewer of the tensions that often come through too frequent bit contact. But for the freedom implied by the loose rein method of riding, be it with an English or a Western bit, the horse must be well schooled and that schooling applied in trail work, not left behind in the manège.

Hackamore

The mechanical hackamore acts like a curb but higher up under the horse's lower jawbone than a bit curb. The principles of use are similar, but make sure it is not fitted too low down as when pressure is applied the noseband could interfere with adequate supplies of oxygen. Do not ride on a constant pressure.

If a bosal is used it should be light, and it is a good idea to alternate the height at which it is fitted by about an inch so that sensitivity is maintained. It can be used either one-handed via neckreining, or two-handed as in snaffle bit riding. The heel knot under the lower jaw should be properly fitted, and the bosal itself should be adjusted neither too tightly, nor slopping about so loosely that it chafes.

Great attention should be paid to the wear on whichever bit is used. Penalties, and in extreme cases elimination, occur if a bit rubs against the horse's mouth (or the curb pinches) and causes laceration. Bit severity should be noted. With a curb this is dictated by several things: the length of shank below the bit; the length of branch above the bit; the tightness of curb; the width of curb chain or leather; the design of mouthpiece; and the thinness of mouthpiece. I do not recommend the ultra-thick so-called 'kind' type of bit, as many horses do not have large enough mouths to take such a bit, and although pressure is spread over a larger area so are the messages which become correspondingly weak and very easy to ignore. It is much better to deliver the message positively and then leave the horse alone than to inflict constant bruising pressure because the initial message does not register.

An endurance horse's reactions and

responses must be quick. Stumbles and wasted energy cost rides, and a rider is doing his horse no kindness in permitting delayed obedience to the bit.

Showing

by Robert Oliver

The art of bitting show horses which go with a high head carriage and are light in the rider's hands has always been a controversial equestrian subject. When bitting for the show ring, always study the horse's mouth carefully. Some, you will see, have large mouths while others are quite small and narrow. Do make sure the bits are carefully fitted and adjusted accordingly. Undue pressure on a large, fleshy tongue will make many horses resist the bit.

The fixed-sided Weymouth of average length shank, together with a reasonably tight curb chain, will give greater control over the majority of horses than the loose, slack curb chain which many people believe is being kind but is really not so. Many horses go much better in the show ring with a covered or leather curb chain. Horses should not be over-bridled, especially when they have to be ridden by many different judges. Always remember, though, that there is quite a difference between riding a horse at home and in the company of, perhaps, twenty others galloping round a large ring.

All riding horses should flex at the poll and give of their lower jaws to the riders' hands and aids. Forced methods are unnecessary and harmful in the extreme. Many horses' mouths are ruined from being lunged in tack with tight side-reins. The badly bitted and unschooled horse will be heavy on the forehand, lean on the rider's hands and be uncomfortable and unbalanced to ride. The happy horse will go forward, balanced and free.

Try to avoid using brand new bits and bridles in the ring until they have been well oiled and used at home, otherwise the leather will be stiff and the bits, in the case of double bridles, do not usually manipulate easily.

It is now possible to purchase darkened leather which is excellent, or even black (which I personally do not like). A well fitted bridle enhances the appearance of the horse. Likewise, a head for the show ring should be dressed to suit its size, as nothing looks more out of place than a fine leather bridle on a big plain head, or vice versa. This point particularly applies to nosebands; a good, wide one will help 'cover up' a plain head.

The Pelham bit is seen more and more in the show ring today, often as a short cut. It attempts to achieve with one mouthpiece what the Weymouth does with two. Theoretically and practically, this is impossible but it is a bit in which many horses go kindly. The mouthpiece is usually half-mooned, being often made of vulcanite and having less pressure on the tongue than a straight-bar bit. Apart from this, the Pelham exerts pressure on the same parts of the head as the Weymouth but only when the curb rein predominates almost exclusively.

Show Hacks

Fortunately, in recent years show hacks have been ridden in less severe bits. In the past, excessively long curbs were in fashion, with many ornate bits having bent cheekpieces. Hacks were always expected to be very light in hand, and many were ridden with a curb bit only. The long-cheeked double bridle with a high port was mainly used.

The late Sam Marsh, a past master of hack showing, always used a Scamperdale Pelham bit. Its main advantage is in having a mouthpiece that turns back at each end, bringing the cheekpieces further to the rear and away from the area of the mouth that often becomes chafed. They are excellent for young horses, being mild, and helping to prevent soreness in the mouth. Pelhams have many advantages for difficult mouths, especially the vulcanite type and the Scamperdale – and they are permitted in the show ring.

A short-cheeked double bridle is now becoming widely used, with hacks taking more contact with the bit. Unfortunately, so many lean on them and are far too strong in their way of going. It was always considered correct for a hack to be ridden with one hand only, the left hand being the bridle hand, leaving the rider (if male) free to raise his hat to a lady or another gentleman, or (if a lady) to blow kisses or wave to her friends.

For four-year-olds and novices, Tom Thumb Weymouths with their very short cheeks are mild in their use, and young horses go kindly in them. I usually experience no difficulty in introducing a horse to the double bridle providing they are going well in a snaffle, and taking a good even contact. I then like to hack them about in the double at home before their first appearance in the ring.

Hunters

Show hunters are expected to go freely forward well into their bridles. Roy Trigg mainly uses a high-ported, steel Pelham bridle on most of his hunters and finds they go well in them; they also suit him and the judge. David Tatlow prefers light, sharp bits and likes his hunters to be very light in the hand.

In the past, many double bridles were well made with lovely stitched-on bits, and horses always appeared to go well in them. I am sure more time and trouble was taken then with the schooling than in recent years. I have witnessed some very severe-looking, narrow, sharp modern bits in the ring of late, which I personally do not like the look of.

Cobs

In the show ring today, we are seeing large numbers of cobs presented. The bitting of the cob is not always as straightforward as one would imagine. With the majority having short, thick necks and independent personalities, they tend to pull and be strong into the gallop. A twisted snaffle together with a fairly long-cheeked Weymouth deals adequately with most strong characters. Some go well in the Banbury curb bit,

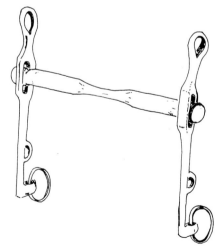

Fig 88   A Banbury curb.

which prevents the animal taking hold and leaning.

For a strong horse, the Swales three-in-one bit will sometimes be seen. It is a form of Pelham and the mouthpiece and cheeks revolve in two rings set round the mouthpiece. There is no poll pressure but considerable curb action can be obtained.

The Rugby Pelham finds favour at the moment with exhibitors, often with a mullen mouthpiece together with a loose ring attached closely to the cheeks (often as a disguise for a double bridle).

In-Hand Show Horses and Ponies

Nothing looks worse than to see in-hand animals with large bits hanging out of their mouths. It is equally important to fit bits correctly, especially in young stock classes, as many young horses' mouths have been ruined by their being shown incorrectly bitted.

I personally prefer a straight bar bit fitted fairly high to prevent any likelihood of animals getting their tongues over the bit, a habit that is very difficult to

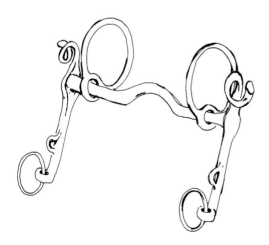

Fig 89   A Swales 3-in-one.

cure when ridden. A straight bar steel or vulcanite snaffle is ideal, but it should not be too wide otherwise it will slip about. A leather coupling fitted to the lead rein is preferred to any type of chain. Only on a stallion, for extra control, should a chain be fitted, running along the chin groove. Yearling fillies and Arab mares are often shown without a bit. Brood-mares can be shown in double bridles or Pelhams.

Showjumping
by Alison Dawes

Bitting and bridling horses is a never-ending subject both for the novice rider and the expert. Because every horse is a little different in some way, be it in conformation, temperament or a mixture of both, and every rider, too, the basic guide to bits is to suit the rider first. There is no point in putting a strong stopping bit, requiring very sensitive handling, on a horse if the rider is not good enough to use it correctly. It would be rather like putting a very powerful car in inexperienced hands. Power is only good when handled with great care, timing, knowledge and experience.

Plain and Jointed Snaffles

The popular feeling in recent years – that the plain snaffle is the perfect bit and all horses and ponies should go in it – is absolute rubbish. If the animal was correctly broken and mouthed in the first place, which unfortunately is unusual these days, it may well have a genuine 'snaffle mouth', but then, if a less capable rider buys the horse or pony and is heavy-handed and unbalanced, leaning on the reins for support and as a way of staying on, the animal quickly develops bad habits trying to evade the extra pressure in its mouth.

The jointed bit becomes more severe when the horse lowers its head too far, or raises it, as the joint of the bit as well as the normal nutcracker action can then either push up into the soft palate or down on to the tongue. This in time will probably make the horse pull its tongue back in an effort to make the bit more comfortable in its mouth. The tongue can then come over the bit, taking away all the cushion it was providing and causing real discomfort and pain, so rendering the animal quite uncontrollable.

A bit I have used a great deal, both for my own horses and in teaching other riders, is the soft rubber snaffle. This big, loose-ringed bit is completely comfortable in the horse's mouth because of its construction and because it is flexible. It wraps round the jaw when extra pressure is exerted and thereby evenly distributes the pressure created by the rider through the reins. The rubber also has a slightly more abrasive surface than the metal bit, and creates more feeling through the lips of the horse. Because the bit is comfortable, and even under great pressure causes no pain or discomfort to the horse, it will respond much more willingly to it. If it is combined with a drop, a Grakle or the more modern flash noseband, it is a most efficient method of control for very many animals and keeps the horse supple at the same time.

All control of the horse is a pattern of signals which are simply different pressures applied to certain areas of the horse's anatomy. A martingale, for example, becomes part of the bridle because it combines with the bit in the horse's mouth to produce the desired balance and reaction between horse and rider by producing different pressures.

Not so many years ago, the normal, and probably the only, bridles you would find hanging in the tack room of an average yard would be a plain mouthed snaffle, a twisted snaffle, a gag and a double bridle, and always a standing martingale. In fact, you could easily drop the twisted snaffle as it is a very sharp bit, and really only works well on a rather hard mouth; in any case, the double bridle would do a much better job. The advantage of the twisted snaffle, of course, means that the rider only has one rein to hold instead of two.

Gags

The gag bridle, again much maligned in recent times simply through ignorance, is again a most effective bridle with which to control the very strong horse and the impetuous horse with rather a light mouth. This may sound surprising, as the general concept of the gag is that it is very sharp and severe, and definitely falls into the category of 'gadget' and is to be avoided. The action is very positive but kind on the mouth; because of the sliding of the bit up the cheeks of the bridle, its effect is never so abrupt, nor so hard on the bars of the mouth, as the plain snaffle.

Pelhams

Pelhams in all forms are once again best used by better riders because they are very positive. The pressure goes on to the bars of the mouth, on the chin groove via the curb chain, and, depending on the length of cheek above the mouthpiece, on the poll, by way of the lever action from the curb rein. In my experience, the Pelham has a tendency to make a horse rather 'wooden', especially when turning.

In general, if all riders learn to ride in the genuine sense of the word, so that they achieve really good balance on the horse and control of their own body without the use of the reins, then everything they do with their hands is quite independent and, therefore, highly controlled and light, and each hand can work quite separately from the other. Once this is achieved, then, while training a horse for competition or actually competing, or in any situation which perhaps fires up the horse more than during routine work, a change of bit, and possibly certain parts of the bridle, can produce almost magically effective results so quickly.

Competition Bitting

The different disciplines in competition, requiring the very highest degree of control at all times, not unnaturally produce the greatest variety in bits and bridles, and I think showjumping has the widest variety of all. There are two main reasons for this, one being that there are very few restrictions on saddlery laid down by either the national or international governing bodies. The major one, which seems unfounded and unnecessary, is the banning of standing martingales in international competitions. Otherwise, every bit, and sometimes a combination of two bits, or one bit and a hackamore, are permissible.

Another reason for top class jumping horses needing bits with a very special action is that during a round of jumping a big course, you need an incredible amount of power from the horse, which cannot be obtained through speed but must be achieved by impulsion, whilst at the same time keeping the horse soft, athletic and very supple.

I often used certain different bits on the same horse, according to the courses, and the size of the arena. Not many horses go in the same bit at Hickstead and Aachen, for example, which are large, open arenas with strongly built, solid-looking fences, as they would at Wembley, a small and confined arena with much lighter poles and airy fences with a lot of daylight showing.

A bit I used regularly for quick control, such as at indoor shows, is the Cornish or Scorrier snaffle. Basically, it is a driving bit but it works beautifully on what I describe as a mature mouth on a horse that likes to go on, and is therefore better suited to the big arenas but not so easy to control in a tight space. The bit is quite sharp and severe, and as long as the horse respects it, and does not fight and run against it, it just produces that extra roundness in the horse, to shorten its stride and keep it bouncy and forward-going at the same time.

Another that has much the same effect but is better still because it is not severe in the mouth at all, is the very popular Tennessee Walking Horse bit. This is relatively new to Britain and was produced originally in the southern states of America for the plantation owners' high stepping, five-gaited horses who are very fiery and Thoroughbred in type and temperament. This long-cheeked lever action bit keeps a horse's head very bent through a very soft jaw while allowing all the freedom of movement through the rest of the body.

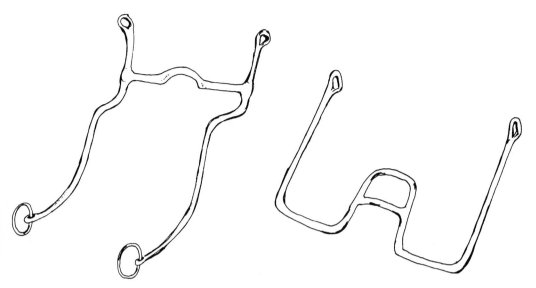

Fig 90   A Walking Horse bit.

Fig 91   A tongue grid/gate.

Tongue Gates

Many horses (riders, too!) become more nervous, a bit tense and excited at competitions or in any other situations that are more exciting than home, such as hunting or even just working with more horses around. This can often change their way of going so that instead of the calm, rhythmic paces you are looking for you are getting a rather staccato beat, which is not smooth or even. In this case, the horse very often draws its tongue up into its throat and, even if the tongue does not come over the bit, it leaves the mouth without its cushion of tongue for the bit to rest on and makes the whole of the neck and throat muscles tight.

There are several types of tongue gate which can be fitted under the bridle and can help enormously in this situation. These consist of a steel mouthpiece with a large port in the middle which should just prevent the tongue from being pulled up into the back of the mouth. Normally,

these gates work perfectly and, once the habit is broken, are only there as a check.

Another very good little attachment is the rubber tongue port which just folds on to the centre of the bit in a loop. One good point about this device is that it then also provides extra padding on a jointed bit, and very often it has been the joint that has been upsetting the horse in the first place.

Conclusion

To take a general look at the bitting and bridling of any horse, consider first the rider, who must have a well balanced, independent seat. Then consider the horse as an individual and decide what is wrong and why. If the problem is a lack of initial training, the horse's age will dictate whether it is best to adapt or reschool to get the best results.

The bits themselves fall into two categories – the strong and the severe. The strong will suit many more horses and riders because the severe ones need such a desperately light touch, and the moment there is too much of something the horse tends to go a bit berserk. The strong bit can be tuned to be more or less so by being used with one or two reins; even on snaffle bits, two reins are more effective than one. Martingales (the length of which completely alters the power of the bit), different types of noseband, leather or metal curb chains – all these items must be skilfully used and adjusted by the horseman under all conditions to get exactly the right amount of pressure at exactly the right moment, while the horse progresses smoothly forwards at all times and answers to the pressures given by the rider quickly and without resistance. This will give the perfect ride and the perfect result on the day.

But there are no short cuts and only time, patience and dedication to learning will bring a rider anywhere near perfection. The better you become the more you realise that there is so much to learn.

The Contributors

Tom Coombes is one of Britain's international carriage driving judges and a noted author on the subject of competition carriage driving. His book *Horse Driving Trials* is regarded as an essential manual by novice and expert competitors alike.

Anthony Crossley. Shortly before *The Horse and the Bit* went to press, news reached us of the death of Lt.-Col. Anthony Crossley. The chapter he contributed to this book is one of the last pieces of work he did and, like all his other writings in both his own books and in articles for equestrian journals, it shows his talent as a writer and his meticulous thought, logic and caring attitude as a horseman.

Tony rode in his youth and during army service. After a break of 25 years, he began riding again, taking particular interest in dressage in which he was almost entirely self-taught, studying all the literature and, as he put it, 'using the old noddle'. An international participator, observer and reporter, his books on the training of the horse will continue to be much sought after and highly regarded for many years.

Alison Dawes is a former international and Olympic competitor in the field of show jumping. She spent several years instructing in this discipline but is now working with a large equestrian retail store on the Welsh borders. Probably her best-known horse was The Maverick.

Antony Dent is a noted equestrian historian and author. He currently lives with his wife in the Dordogne in France, where he has a small farm and works as a translator.

Ron Etherington is Managing Director of James Cotterell and Sons Limited, one of the oldest-established companies in Britain producing saddlery hardware and fittings for the leather goods industry. The company manufactures the Kangaroo range of bits and equestrian products.

Rod Fisher is a partner in a busy general veterinary practice in Abergavenny, specialising in the equine side of the practice. He is active in all aspects of competitive riding.

Stella Harries takes great pleasure in starting off young animals on their showing careers, a skill for which she is particularly known. She acts as an advisor for owners seeking show animals. One of her happiest memories is of winning the Winston Churchill Cup with Ridgewood Venture at the Royal International Horse Show.

Charles Harris was the first English rider to complete the full three-year graduation course at The Spanish Riding School of Vienna. He is much in demand as an instructor and equestrian author of books, pamphlets and magazine articles, his *Fundamentals of Riding* being the official manual of the Association of British Riding Schools.

Jane Holderness-Roddam is a former Olympic and international three-day event competitor and author of many books and articles on equestrian topics. She competes and also instructs and lectures internationally. She lives with her husband on their farm in Wiltshire. She is also a member of the three-day event Selection Committee.

Ann Hyland is a successful and experienced international competitor in long distance and endurance rides, having won awards in America, Australia and Germany. In Britain, she has won many top awards. She is a noted equestrian author and exponent of English and Western riding. Although she no longer breeds endurance horses from her own mares, her well-known stallion, Nizzolan, continues to produce them from mares visiting the author's stud in Cambridgeshire.

Dorothy Johnson maintains that one of her most enjoyable equestrian experiences was being behind the scenes at Aldershot in 1948 when she was able to watch the different teams preparing their horses for the Olympic Games. Linked for many years with the Northern Equitation Centre at Aughton, she now enjoys independence and great popularity helping people train their horses for varied disciplines. She herself has competed in many spheres, including Grade A show jumping and point-to-point racing.

Dési Lorent was for many years an airline pilot. During that time, he spent most of his spare time studying in Portugal under Master Nuno Oliveira, the greatest classical rider of this century. Capt. Lorent daily teaches and practises those classical principles at his establishment in Devon.

Jennie Loriston-Clarke is one of Britain's international dressage competitors, her best-known horse to date probably being the now retired Dutch Courage. She and her husband breed and produce competition horses successful in many spheres, at the Catherston Stud in Hampshire.

Susan McBane has been an equestrian writer for 19 years, specialising in care and management. She has had many years' experience of riding and looking after her own and other people's horses and ponies in all circumstances. She was founder and editor of *Equi* magazine and is secretary of the Equine Behaviour Study Circle.

Robert Oliver is one of Britain's foremost professional show horse producers and exhibitors. Also a respected dealer, he lives with his wife in Gloucestershire. His books and articles on equestrian topics, particularly showing, are much appreciated by a wide readership.

Molly Sivewright and her family own the Talland School of Equitation in Gloucestershire. She is a member of the British Horse Society Council, its Training and Examinations Committee, and the Pony Club Training Committee. She is an international judge and trainer and has ridden with the British dressage team. She is author of two books, *Thinking Riding, Books 1 and 2.*

Sylvia Stanier worked for many years with the Hume Dugeon family in Ireland and during that time was able to expand her equestrian education to cover a very wide variety of systems of equitation and schools of equestrian thought. She is particularly noted for her expertise in classical equitation and in working horses from the ground, and her books are much in demand among discerning riders everywhere.

Moyra Williams worked for many years as a clinical psychologist and has always found it particularly fascinating to combine her professional knowledge with her love of horses. She is author of several books on the psychological aspects of horses, is chairman of the Equine Behaviour Study Circle and breeds competition horses at her farm in Buckinghamshire.

Index